WHAT'S ETHICS GOT TO DO WITH IT?

The Role of Ethics in Undergraduate, Graduate, and Professional Education at Saint Louis University

What's Ethics Got to Do with It?

The Role of Ethics in Undergraduate, Graduate, and Professional Education at Saint Louis University

Edited by

John F. Kavanaugh, S.J.

and

Donna J. Werner

ST. LOUIS: SAINT LOUIS UNIVERSITY PRESS
xxxx

Library of Congress Cataloging-in-Publication Data

What's ethics got to do with it? : the role of ethics in undergraduate, graduate, and professional education at Saint Louis University / edited by John F. Kavanaugh and Donna J. Werner.
    p.cm.
Collection of papers presented at a conference held on May 11, 1999, at Saint Louis University. Included bibliographical references and index.
ISBN 0-9652929-4-0
1. St. Louis University–Congresses. 2. Ethics–Study and Teaching (Higer)–Missouri–Saint Louis–Congresses. 3. College teachers–Professional ethics–Missouri–Saint Louis–Congresses. I. Kavanaugh, John F. II. Werner, Donna J., 1958-

BJ68.S7 W48 2000
174–dc21

                        00-039051

Distribution:

Fordham University Press
2546 Belmont Avenue
University Box L
Bronx NY 10458

CONTENTS

ESSAYS

APPENDICES

PREFACE

The Ethics Across the Curriculum program at Saint Louis University was started at the initiative of faculty members who hoped to integrate their personal lives with the virtues of integrity and compassion in their professions, and a commitment to justice in society. Once formed, the first impulse of the EAC program was to bring together a community of professional scholars who would share with other faculty the various ways they embody an ethical worldview, in the Catholic and Jesuit tradition.

This publication is an effort to enhance the conversation that might occur among a faculty at a major Jesuit university. Universities are so large, we often do not even know what is happening on our own campus. There are networks to be exploited, centers to be used, and programs to be employed. More important than all of this, there are men and women to be met, co-workers and comrades to be seen and heard, friends to be engaged. This book serves, especially, the last concern.

To be sure, we wish to know what is happening in the various graduate programs, the schools, and the undergraduate curriculum. And to a great extent, the articles presented here address this desire— although a more thoroughgoing account will be welcomed in the future. What might be more significant, however, is encountering the kind of men and women we work with. Invariably, it will be a confirmation of our lives and labors as a community of scholars.

But we are not only a community of scholars. We are a moral community. In terms which any humanist may welcome, we are concerned with the authentic flourishing of the individual person, and we know that such flourishing happens only in relationship and in acknowledgment of our solidarity as persons.

Although not all of us are Catholic or even Christian, and certainly few of us are Jesuit, the vision of Ignatius of Loyola illuminates, mysteriously perhaps, much of what we share. We are a people of discernment and community. We seek the liberty of our minds and hearts. We realize that this is tested out only in our relationships. And we know that we are connected to every mother's child. We share, finally, the conviction that all of our gifts and efforts must be eventually measured against the standard of truth, which is the only ground for love and commitment.

Conscious of the gift of our being together as professional scholars and teachers at Saint Louis University, the Ethics Across the Curriculum Program called together fourteen of our faculty to speak of the moral dimensions of their professional labors. Over 100 faculty came together to hear their confreres articulate their ethical visions.

To be sure, there is diversity in what we bring to our lives together. More surprisingly is the communality we share.

Our Keynote Presentation was offered by the provost of Saint Louis University, Sandra Johnson, nationally recognized for her work in health care law. The universal response to her lecture on "The Interface of Law, Medicine, and Ethics" was the wish that there had been more time, perhaps the entire morning, set aside for response and discussion among the gathered philosophers, scientists, theologians, nurses, physicians, physical therapists, and administrators. Sandra Johnson, incontestably committed to the inherent dignity of human life, raised the issue of pain in the face of death. In an elegant account of the legal and medical challenges to pain management, she rooted her challenge to contemporary opinion in a profound sensibility to human suffering and intrinsic human worth. As a lawyer, sympathetic to physicians, and personally involved in the suffering of our most vulnerable, Professor Johnson calls every professional to personal integrity, interpersonal care, and social responsibility.

Gerard Magill's portrayal of "Ethics in Health Sciences Education" is a most appropriate beginning to the conversation. Although directly concerned with health care, his offering of independence, inter-dependence, and influence as value hallmarks, each characterized by strategic virtues, should be welcomed by any university school or department. It is an analysis, we shall see, that truly reaches across the entire curriculum.

While the case study approach which James Fisher uses in courses of business ethics does overtly articulate standards or virtues required for morally acceptable practice, the elicited responses from students as well as the quandaries faced by businesspersons provide a subtle inter-weaving and contrasting of individuality, collaboration, and social sensibility found in the Magill presentation. The very notion of pro-fessional responsibility rests upon the haunting presence of ethics in every arena of life.

Dennis Tuchler, while recommending that a personal ethical distance be held in the professional relationship, not only acknowledges the ethical component of legal education but also provides a concrete example of suggestive case studies and probing questions from his own Thomas Deline Program on Ethics for Entering Law Students.

In the College of Public Service, James Gilsinan suggests how Magill's third hallmark of influence touches upon the university's relationship to the community at large. This is concretely exemplified in the college's interaction with the local Saint Louis citizenry in issues of diversity, public space, and political organization. While focused on the social dimension of ethics, there is, nonetheless a strong undercurrent emphasis on personal integrity as well as "companionship," an inter-dependence crucial to catalytic leadership.

Sharon Homan reveals how the School of Public Health complements many of the themes in Gilsinan's approach. The "hermeneutic circle of experience, reflection, and action" penetrates every sphere of our lives—as professional, as private person, as public activist. Thus, professional ethics is mirrored in the ethics of the professional wherein the claims of individual autonomy and character formation, the common interest and social obligation are unified in the notion of covenant. She models this theory in her examination of programs and projects in the School of Public Health.

Psychologist James Korn, from the Center for Teaching Excellence, examines the actual ethics of teaching, especially in the context of student-professor relationships. Korn offers astute observations on the most commonplace of quandaries that teachers encounter in their ordinary professional lives—not as scholars primarily, but as covenanted advisors, exemplars, instructors, and colleagues. The web of personal integrity, mutuality, and social solidarity thus weaves together, once again, our lives.

The afternoon presenters, all teachers of undergraduates, under-standably moved to the concrete arena of teacher-student encounter.

Michael Barber offers a philosophical interpretation, from the phenomenological tradition, of our relationships with students as "other," in all their diversity and individuality as well as their shared experience as the receivers of education. Using an "optics" metaphor, on Barber's account, ethics is a lens through which we approach, in reverence, the truth—not to impose our view of reality, but to call forth the reality in the face of the other present before us.

Mark Chmiel, an adjunct professor in Theological Studies, reminds us of other faces than those of the academic world. They are encountered in the acts of personal wonder, felt tragedy, and ethical passion. Sensitive to the poverties of our students, we are provided the opportunity to lead students, in accompaniment, to be sensitive to the poor. This is done not only through instruction and through encounter of the great culturally adversarial lives of Dorothy Day, Ignatius Ellacuria, Martin Luther King, and Oscar Romero, but also through the lived engagement of the poor of our own city. The pain of recognizing the immiseration of people around us elicits our own acknowledged vulnerability. The ethical imperative is applied not only to the world, but to ourselves.

Judith Gibbons, as psychologist and pioneer in women's studies, assiduously and courageously investigates those vulnerabilities that our students encounter in themselves and which we must attend to. The particular stage of development where most university students find themselves requires a heightened sensibility from faculty. And yet our empathy for the life struggle of our younger collaborators must extend to our peers. They too, professional and possibly tenured notwith-standing, call forth the very solidarity which our students long for.

In Joya Uraizee's teaching of undergraduate English, we find a striking application of Barber's philosophy and Gibbons's psychology. Post-Colonial literature, from Nigeria to Pakistan to the Caribbean, elicits from all of us an experience of human solidarity with the aspirations of autonomy, relationship, and social significance. The phenomenon of moral evil need not be pursued in the textbook; it is present in the social (and even the educational) structures of ethnocentric, class, and racial stereotyping.

Robert Bolla unfolds not only a social world, but a universe which is charged with value and ethical urgency. The revolution in biological, agricultural, and biomedical sciences of the last two decades catches our breath. Bolla masterfully recounts the emergent challenges in isolating, cloning, and sequencing genomes of various organisms. There is almost an inevitable imperative to research anything which might heighten human flourishing and lessen our impoverishments. These awesome challenges, however, are subtly mirrored in the day-by-day ethical challenges of students who write reports, are tempted to plagiarism, and are lured to cheating. These pedestrian quandaries exhibit the same challenge that we face in scientific research and methodology. Integrity is a personal and a professional virtue; honesty, a private and a social benefit. The new biology may raise many novel ethical issues, but the patterns of resolution will require the same discernment and wisdom that the living of our daily and professional lives ask of us.

Avis Meyer's reflections provide, in his own words, an apt strategy "to conclude this symposium," and to summarize the efforts of a faculty with its curriculum to welcome and name the ethical dimension of our lives. His chosen optic is compassion, a lens which brings into focus the most interior realms of our private lives, the most intense exchanges of intimacy and relationship, the most strategic concerns of our social and political commitments. His mode of discourse is the story. And all the narratives are of former students, men and women who had a sense of their deepest selves which led them beyond themselves, who found in the face of the other the face of our compassionate God, who in their eventual professional lives took measures to lessen the suffering of the world.

These gifts which we find in so many of our students and graduates reveal what we are, ultimately, about. They uncover our ultimate concern. They embody for us what "ethics across the curriculum" means. They may also suggest why, in God's kind favor, we have been drawn together.

John F. Kavanaugh, S.J.

ACKNOWLEDGMENTS

This book would not be possible without the help and support of a number of people. First and foremost, we'd like to thank all those who contributed to our inaugural conference—both the presenters (whose papers are contained in this volume) as well as the enthusiastic attendees who participated in the discussions. We're especially indebted to Provost Sandra Johnson for an engaging keynote address and Dr. Vallee Willman, M.D. for moderating the discussion that no one wanted to end. We're also grateful to Dean Patricia Monteleone for her support in making the morning session at the Medical School possible.

We would like to thank all those involved with the formation of the Ethics Across the Curriculum Program at Saint Louis University. The program began as an ad hoc committee of volunteers from various disciplines, including Maria Bartlett (Social Work), Paul Czysz (Engineering), Mary Domahidy (Public Policy), Paul Duffy, S.J. (Communication), James E. Fisher (Business), Garth Hallett, S.J. (Philosophy and Letters), Sharon Homan (Public Health), Ed Lisson, S.J. (Theological Studies), Gerard Magill (Center for Health Care Ethics), Kevin O'Rourke, O.P. (Center for Health Care Ethics), Vince Punzo (Philosophy), Lars Reuter, S.J. (Theological Studies), Doris Rubio (Research Methodology), Roy Ruckdeschel (Social Work), William Shea (Theological Studies), Dennis Tuchler (Law School), and Theodore Vitali, C.P. (Philosophy). This group, with the support of Richard Breslin and Michael Garanzini, S.J., made the program a reality. We also appreciate the advice and encouragement we received from Thomas Shanks, S.J., Executive Director of the Markkula Center for Applied Ethics at Santa Clara University, and Robert Ashmore, Director of the Center for Ethics Studies at Marquette University. We're especially grateful to Fr. Ted Vitali, C.P., who chaired the initial committee and has continued to play a key role in the development of the program.

We've continued to benefit from the contribution of many of these individuals as they have remained committed to the program as members of our Advisory Committee. Over time, they have been joined by Michael Barber, S.J. (Philosophy), Cynthia Cook (Social Work), Shirley Dowdy (Arts & Sciences), James Gilsinan (Public Service), Ellen Harshman (Provost Office), Ann Hayes (Physical Therapy), Mary Elizabeth Hogan (Arts & Sciences), Sandra Johnson (Provost Office),

William Keenan (Medical School), J. J. Mueller, S.J. (Theological Studies), John Pauly (Communication), Peter Salsich (Law School), Deirdre Schweiss (Nursing School), Diane Walters (Professional Studies), and Vallee Willman (Medical School). The Ethics Across the Curriculum Program indeed owes its success to its Advisory Committee. We are most fortunate to work with this group of dedicated, talented professionals—all strategic to the mission of Saint Louis University— and we continue to be amazed at their generosity, wisdom, and commitment.

We appreciate the hard work and support of the professionals at The University of Scranton Press (Richard W. Rousseau, S.J., Patricia Mecadon, and Trinka Ravaioli) and at Saint Louis University Press (Dean Donald Brennan, Carol Murphy, and especially our astute copy-editor, Mary Waldron). We are most grateful to our president, Fr. Lawrence Biondi, S.J., for his continued commitment to ethics across the curriculum. And, finally, we'd like to thank Fr. A. James Blumeyer, S.J., and the Marchetti Jesuit Endowment Fund without whom the Ethics Across the Curriculum Program at Saint Louis University would not exist.

THE INTERFACE OF LAW, MEDICINE, AND ETHICS

Sandra H. Johnson
Saint Louis University

Working in an intersection—whether it be Grand Avenue and Caroline or the intersection of law, medicine, and ethics—is often treacherous. We lawyers, physicians, philosophers, and theologians each come to the intersection of law, medicine, and ethics with quite different training. Our distinct training has included a deep socialization that often leads to totally disparate perceptions of events and relationships. Even simple words carry potential for miscommunication as the same word may carry entirely different meanings or connotations within our own disciplines. We could have a revealing exercise for our time together today if we were simply to discuss what we each mean when we say something "caused" something else or what we each mean when we say we "know" something.

One of the risks of working in an interdisciplinary field is that you must tread on the fields of others and you risk being named an arrogant trespasser. We are all familiar with such charges: that the philosopher is pretending to be a lawyer, that the lawyer is playing the role of doctor, and that the doctor thinks he has an inside track to understanding God. And within our own "home" disciplines, we can be charged with that terrible crime of working in a merely "applied" arm of the field and diluting disciplinary rigor.

Despite what might be viewed as hazardous duty on a number of fronts, I have found working within law, medicine, and ethics to be a rich experience—rich because the issues are compelling and central to the human experience; rich, too, because the questions raised are ones that make us examine meaning and value in life. The heart of interdisciplinary work is asking questions and challenging professional and disciplinary assumptions. This makes it intellectually challenging and creative. With experience, we learn to listen closely and carefully and to stay at the table even when it appears that there is no common language. At its best, bioethics teaches humility—humility before the quietly heroic human beings we find both among the professionals and among the patients and families. It also should teach modesty before the

1

nature of the questions that are put center stage—questions that simply are not satisfied by easy answers.

Generalizations about the intersection of medicine, law, and ethics, however, cannot fully capture the dynamic among the professions. Examining a particular problem or case study is more informative. In this presentation, I want to talk about the intersection of law, medicine, and ethics through the lens of pain relief. Working through some of the current problems presented in the effort to provide adequate pain relief will serve as a vehicle for examining several fundamental and pervasive issues in bioethics. These are:

1. The relevance of actual medical custom and practice to the determination of what is ethical;
2. The relation of legal norms and risks to the determination of ethical duties in medicine; and
3. The consequences of "legalizing" principles of ethics or moral theology.

A central focus of bioethics is the quest to bring medical practice, legal norms, and ethical duties into harmony. Clinical ethics, law, and medical practice should be "on the same page" in most cases. Where conflict or contradiction among the three occurs it is viewed as something that requires change—either change in the ethical paradigm or its application, or change in the law, or change in medical practice. Still, because ethics and law are normative and because they sometimes proceed from different principles, some tension and conflict with practice is to be expected. Each of the three issues listed above presents an opportunity to explore the differences between law and medicine and ethics within the context of pain relief.

Treatment of Pain in the United States

The medical capacity to relieve pain is greater than it has ever been. Effective pain management is medically available for cancer pain, for pain related to diseases at the end of life, and for chronic, nonmalignant pain. Effective pain management is available in many forms, including opioids, which have proven effective for both cancer pain and non-cancer chronic pain. Most pain, including most cancer pain, can be relieved through relatively simple means.

The ethical duty to relieve pain is very well established. Although there may be ethical or medical concerns about particular interventions at the outer limits, the core ethical obligation to relieve avoidable pain is not subject to great dispute.

Yet pain continues to be seriously neglected and undertreated in the United States. Treatable but untreated pain is a widespread problem that cuts across all patient populations. The problem is well documented, and the empirical research on neglected pain is consistent and uniform whether the research is focusing on pain at the end of life, pain associated with cancer, chronic pain, sickle cell pain, or pain in children and the elderly. Moreover, elderly, minorities, women, children, and those unable to speak for themselves due to disability bear a disproportionate burden of ineffective or neglectful treatment for pain. Despite the development of effective and inexpensive pain management interventions and the overall human and financial cost, pain is neglected and undertreated in the United States.

Why does undertreatment of pain persist even though we have the capacity to relieve pain safely and even though it is an ethical duty of the first order? The reasons emerge from all sides. They are cultural, educational, medical, and legal.

Although I will discuss the ethical, legal, and medical issues in more detail, it should be understood that some of the problem lies in the patients themselves. Attitudes in our own culture relating to the redemptive power of pain ("no pain, no gain" or "offer it up") and to an aversion to signs of "weakness" may contribute to our suspicion of reports of pain and to the hesitation of patients to advocate for themselves. In addition, especially for older generations, a distrust of "drugs" and the overwhelming public image of drug users as criminals and outcasts may cause patients to resist effective medication. Beyond patients' and caregivers' attitudes and general and specific cultural attributes, however, there are problems in the delivery of pain relief within the health professions and within health care institutions.

Serious deficiencies in medical and nursing training and education form a significant obstacle to effective pain relief. Several efforts are underway to increase training of doctors and nurses in the assessment and treatment of pain. Part of the problem in medical and nursing education, however, is that much of the research on the effectiveness and safety of certain drugs for pain relief is relatively recent and contradicts the "common knowledge" of earlier medical practices. As evidenced by empirical research on patterns of medical practices, physicians learn most effectively and adapt their practice patterns in response to their observations of the practice and the mentoring of colleagues rather than new information delivered in any other educational format. This method of learning means that clinical knowledge, especially as it relates to evaluation and technique, can be very slow to diffuse among the practice and can meet active resistance. It also means that efforts focused only on formal education may be too limited because they are so easily undone by physicians in the practice. This appears to be the case with efforts to change treatment decision making regarding pain management.

Institutional policies and practices can also create barriers to access. Once again, there are efforts to improve this situation, including the recent inclusion of pain management in national accreditation standards for hospitals, but institutions that have worked on removing barriers to pain relief have found it difficult to change deeply held attitudes that underlie the undertreatment of pain.

One reason for the undertreatment of pain identified by physicians is the threat of legal sanctions for treating patients in pain, especially when that treatment must rely on the use of controlled substances. Studies of physician attitudes and practices repeatedly indicate that physicians behave more conservatively in their prescribing practices for fear of legal action, particularly disciplinary action. There is substantial evidence that the state medical boards and other enforcement agencies responsible for regulating the use of controlled substances have been guided primarily by the "war on drugs." Recognition of the duty to relieve pain has been far in the background. Although fear of the law on the part of physicians may be overblown in other contexts, it appears to be based in a realistic assessment of risk in regard to the prescription of adequate pain medications.

Here, too, significant change has taken place in the regulatory environment in the last three years. State medical boards are adjusting their standards on prescribing practices to reflect current research and to focus on pain relief, and several states have established "pain commissions" to assess and improve the delivery of pain management. Whether these relatively recent efforts will produce real change depends on whether regulatory investigative and enforcement practices will actually conform to the new standards. Change in physicians' perception of legal risk will require some passage of time to overcome the rather prominent anti-drug efforts of the past two decades.

So, we have a paradox in the area of pain relief. We *can* and we *should* relieve pain, but we don't. The reasons are varied. They include deeply held values on the part of patients and health care professionals, institutional obstacles, and barriers erected by the legal system. There currently is a strong movement to remove barriers to effective medical treatment of pain. Some of the issues revealed in the disjunction among capacity and desire and practice in pain management lead to an examination of some of the basic questions that arise at the convergence of law, medicine, and ethics.

The Relevance of Medical Custom

Both law and bioethics, as applied sciences, must constantly deal with context. Legal and ethical norms for medicine must be tested in the clinical context, in the arena of actual practices. Both ordinarily should pass the hurdle of "workability." Bioethics that is not grounded in the clinical setting is irrelevant at best, and at worst can be harmful to the quality of care and to the physician-patient relationship.

The understanding of bioethics as fundamentally an applied field has stimulated a very serious and growing body of empirical research on the actual "practice" of clinical ethics. For example, the Robert Wood Johnson Foundation sponsored a multi-year, multi-institutional, and multimillion-dollar study on end-of-life care which tested physician compliance with the ethical and legal norms of patient decision making (informed consent) in medical care at the end of life. This study, named SUPPORT, found that physicians generally did not know of their patients' wishes and made decisions that did not reflect their patients' choices.

Now, over two decades since the Quinlan case, and with so little change effected by the full-court press of the SUPPORT study, we might conclude that the problem is not entirely an issue of physician misbehavior or resistance. Rather, if such meager results persist over so long a time, one might suspect that "first principles" of the modern physician-patient relationship would be at risk of abandonment. In ethics, and most forcefully in American law, the fundamental principle has been that the individual patient's choice and his or her identity, values, and religious beliefs should determine the course of medical treatment. Perhaps the empirical research that reveals how far practice is from that principle proves we should abandon those principles and allow physicians to make decisions in the best interest of the patient without direct participation by the patient. Perhaps the norms of patient and family decision making at the end of life are wrongheaded since it apparently is not being practiced regularly after two decades of legal and educational efforts. Similarly, the persistent evidence of neglect of pain relief could be construed as a measure of the ethical and legal principles supporting adequate pain management.

But the universal reaction to the SUPPORT study was not to reject the ethical principles. It was instead a nationwide effort to do better by those first principles. Why the persistence? It may simply be the American culture's steadfast devotion to individuality. I think it is that and more. The adherence to these, and other, principles despite disappointing levels of noncompliance reflects another view of the character of bioethics that is in tension with the recognition of the importance of context.

As much as bioethics seeks détente among its constituent elements, it is incontrovertibly in a state of tension. This tension springs directly from an assertion that ethics and law are normative and not merely descriptive. That the profession of medicine fosters a particular practice does not make that practice ethical. Similarly, the legality of an act does not on its own determine whether the act is ethical. Neither is the law the handmaiden of medicine. Sometimes, though not too frequently, the law should establish a norm that is different from customary medical practice.

Medicine is a profession, and as such it has enjoyed a singular deference to its authority to establish norms of practice. Traditionally, medicine has been viewed as a profession with a primary duty to ethical behavior. It can be argued, in fact, that medicine has itself generated the most fundamental ethical principles of medical practice, including the fiduciary character of the physician-patient relationship and informed consent. Most areas of medical law do refer to medical practice and custom as the source of legal standards; for example, in medical malpractice law, the actual custom and practice of the medical profession form the legal standard of care in almost all circumstances. Still, the courts from time to time have established standards that are not reflected in the customary medical practice of the time, although they are usually careful to show some evidence of acceptance of the norm in at least some quarters of the medical profession. Actual medical practice is not the ultimate test of ethical and legal norms even though law and ethics both lack sufficient force to effect involuntary compliance in the face of widespread passive resistance.

The debate over the relative influence of aspiration and practice, though an old debate both in law and ethics, is being pressed now for at least two reasons. As discussed previously, the recent emergence of a body of substantial empirical research on the operation of bioethics in practice has given the question an urgency beyond the theoretical. Second, the very public debate over the legalization of assisted suicide has thrown the spotlight on the relationship between ethics, law, and medicine. The emphasis on empirical research as a source of answers for bioethics is quite apparent in some aspects of the recent debate over the legalization of assisted suicide. Research on physician and nurse attitudes and practices, much of it deficient in design, is offered in support of legalization with the argument that such research proves that physician-assisted suicide is practiced and, therefore, is ethical and should be legal.

In the ordinary course of the debate, it is argued that doctors will be the protectors of patient choice and will adequately treat pain. In contrast to the question of what is ethical, this question of how doctors will behave is sociological or psychological and appropriately empirical. The research that reveals that physicians do not know or abide by their patients' choices and that physicians may actually withdraw from patients in pain or from dying patients is, therefore, quite relevant. Proponents of legalization of physician-assisted suicide often seem to ignore the rather substantial empirical evidence that repeatedly and uniformly indicates that physicians do not abide by patient choice and that patients do not receive adequate pain relief even where it is readily available.

Legal Risks and Ethical Duties

Doctors tell us that they neglect pain. They report that one significant reason for this behavior is that the legal risk is too high. The law makes them practice bad medicine, and the threat of disciplinary action or other legal sanction makes them let their patients suffer.

As a lawyer working with health care professionals, I do hear this complaint with some frequency in a variety of contexts, and I usually feel compelled to investigate. At times, the "law" identified is not law at all but rather internal institutional or payor requirements. The insurer or hospital, for example, has a policy that is not required by law but is treated as though it is even though the actual motivation for the rule is risk management or cost control. At other times, the law does not require or prohibit a certain activity but rather only requires reporting or advance authorization. In these circumstances, the legal system may be used as a scapegoat for decisions that relate more to the provider's financial well-being.

In pain management, the complaint that the law requires bad medicine is especially prevalent when the treatment modality is the prescription of controlled substances. In investigating the impact of regulatory oversight of prescribing practices, we discovered that the fear of legal sanctions was a fear grounded in reality. Actual disciplinary penalties for prescribing controlled substances for pain relief are infrequent, but the investigative and enforcement process is prosecutorial and criminal in nature. The cost of being investigated is so high in personal, financial, and professional terms that physicians stay well within acceptable boundaries. Charting a course that is risk-free results in inadequate treatment for pain as physicians avoid prescribing otherwise indicated controlled substances. In addition, we found that the state medical boards were using standards that did not reflect good medical practice and research in pain management. Over the past two to three years, significant progress has been made in reforming the standards, and the Federation of State Medical Boards has issued model guidelines to help the state boards to devise better standards.

The relation of legal risk to ethical duty in the context of the prescription of controlled substances for pain relief raises at least two issues that reach beyond that particular situation. Each issue presents a significant challenge to the role of law in medicine and bioethics.

As a lawyer, I would argue that legal oversight of medical practice, whether through litigation or regulation, is necessary. There are physicians who are "bad actors" and who overprescribe or simply deal drugs. With physicians' hypersensitivity to legal risk in the pain-relief context, however, the law faces a significant challenge. How does the system continue its obligation to monitor the practice and protect the public without causing patients to suffer? Law has an obligation, of course, to assure that good medicine is reflected in the legal standards. Indeed, the focus of efforts to reform the legal process as it applies to this context has been to reformulate standards. Regulatory processes must also be used ethically in terms of proportionality, for example. But that may simply not be enough to comfort physicians.

Physician practices can be shaped quite effectively, as has been proven in managed care, without prohibiting anything. Simply requiring additional paperwork, reporting, justification, or pretreatment review can deter a rational physician from a particular course of treatment. It is understandable that rational physicians may decide to withhold appropriate intervention because of the burden of justifying their recommendation or dealing with a bureaucracy, but it is not ethical to do so. Such behavior violates the primary fiduciary duty to the patient in favor of the doctor's self-interest. It may sound cavalier for a lawyer to say that the physician's primary ethical duty to the patient is the same in this case, although it must be said. In rare circumstances, conscientious objection and civil disobedience arise where the law requires or prohibits an activity the physician views as either immoral or ethically obligatory.

Just as legal norms are not defined entirely by the practice and custom of medicine, law cannot necessarily answer the question of ethical duty in medicine. It does not follow, however, that ethical or moral principles can always be codified as law.

"Legalization" of Ethical Principles

It might be said that the measure of good law is whether it conforms to ethical principles, and this ordinarily would be true. The question of the legalization of assisted suicide and its relationship to the provision of adequate pain relief, however, illustrates a situation in which the legalization of a very important ethical principle would not be desirable.

One need only to remember back to stories in our families—stories of family members screaming or crying in pain because it was not yet "time" for administering the next dose of pain medication—to know the horror of unrelieved suffering and the desperation it causes. The trauma is suffered not only by the patient but also by those who survive being a caregiver in such a circumstance. And you only have to experience once the precious gift of dying without fear of suffering to know that it can unlock the spiritual character of the experience for the dying person and for the family.

The principle of double effect is one of the most important foundational norms in care of the dying. The theological principle of double effect is well known among all who care for terminally ill patients. The principle holds that treating a patient for pain is moral, even if death is among the foreseeable outcomes of the intervention, so long as the intent of the physician or nurse is to relieve pain through an intervention reasonably designed to do so. I view this principle as analogous to many of the calculations that are made each day in medicine—the intervention (say surgery, for example) has known outcomes (including death and disability for some patients). There is a risk of death, but if the benefit outweighs the risk, we go forward.

The principle of double effect is a striking statement, made more so because it is a theological principle recognized by the Catholic Church. The Church has had a tremendous influence on the law of end-of-life care, and its devotion to the protection of human life is well known. For this Church to state that your obligation to relieve pain is so great that the risk of an earlier death is acceptable is powerful.

This principle of double effect has even been recognized in law. The United States Supreme Court in its opinion on assisted suicide, where it found that there was no constitutional right to assisted suicide, cited the principle of double effect as being recognized in state law. Many states with living will statutes include in their statutory living will form a statement in which the patient directs the doctor to provide pain relief even if it may hasten death. It is available as a defense in malpractice actions.

Of course, there are limitations and nuances in the application of double effect. The principle was stated in hypothetical terms over 40 years ago. It is so commonly used that it has become almost a mantra: provide medical care to ease pain *even if it may hasten death*. The reference to death is a hypothetical statement, but it has been so ingrained in the training of nurses and doctors that it has been taken as a statement of fact. Medical care, medical interventions, medication to ease pain at the end of life, may hasten death. Relieving pain hastens death. Although the principle of double effect supports aggressive pain relief, it has also helped to convince doctors and nurses and patients that medicating for pain relief causes death. Of course, there may be a risk of earlier death in certain cases; however, the research and the pharmacological analysis prove that just the opposite is ordinarily true. Medication, such as morphine, for someone in pain at the end of life may in fact prolong life.

The second problem with the double effect principle is that it relies on the intent of the individual doctor or nurse. If the intent is to relieve pain but not to hasten death, the principle applies. In some situations where the illness has been prolonged or the condition is seriously burdensome, we *are* hoping for death, the ultimate relief from suffering and illness. We *would* like death to come sooner rather than later. In working through the dying process, one hopes that the family and patient will reach a point where they are able to let go. It is not at all unusual for patients and families and doctors and nurses to explicitly say that "it's time" and that the patient may be better off if death came.

As a principle of ethics or theology, double effect leaves the examination of conscience and the testing of intent to the individual. If intent becomes an issue in a legal case, for example, in a prosecution for homicide for a death "caused" by the pain medication, it is quite possible that there will be a mix of evidence. We can make good and rational arguments for the centrality of intent as a matter of ethics or morality, but this is the Achilles' heel of the principle of double effect as it takes form in the legal context.

Even with these limitations, the principle of double effect is important and makes a critical contribution to improving care of the dying. In any debate on the ethics or morality of assisted suicide, double effect provides a demarcation between what is ethical and what is not.

In law, double effect is available as a defense to malpractice actions because it reflects the medical standard of care.

In 1998, however, there was a bill in Congress to make assisted suicide a violation of federal drug law. The intention of the proposed statute was to block the implementation in Oregon of that state's statute legalizing assisted suicide. The proposed federal legislation prohibited the use of controlled substances for euthanasia using the federal Controlled Substances Act as the source of the prohibition. Efforts to make assisted suicide and euthanasia affirmatively criminal through explicit criminal statutes will always raise very serious concerns over the impact that this might have on the availability of pain relief to terminally ill patients. The federal bill, therefore, specifically protected interventions that could be justified under the double effect principle.

You could infer from my earlier discussion of assisted suicide and empirical research that I oppose the legalization of assisted suicide. You would be right. It would seem natural then that legislative efforts to make assisted suicide illegal would receive my support, especially since I am so enamored with double effect. Yet I would not offer such support.

Legalization of the ethical and moral principle of double effect in a statute that would make assisted suicide a federal crime would, I believe, cause serious unintended harm to patients and their families. Incorporating the double effect principle into this federal law, within the jurisdiction of the federal Controlled Substances Act, likely would have the perverse effect of stimulating doctors to avoid prescribing the drugs altogether to the detriment of their patients. As discussed earlier, physicians are hypersensitive to regulation regarding the prescription of controlled substances for pain relief, partly as a result of our 20-year war on drugs and the prosecutorial emphasis it established. In addition, the principle of double effect is described in the proposed statute as a potential affirmative defense. The physician or nurse who is charged with euthanasia or assisted suicide in the context of prescribing or administering pain medication would have the burden of proving that his or her actions fell within the confines of double effect. As discussed earlier, a significant limitation of double effect is the inherent and practical difficulty of proving "pure" intent. Thus, the assurance intended by the inclusion of the affirmative defense of double effect is at best completely illusory and at worst a signal to physicians that pain relief for terminally ill patients is a high legal-risk area.

Conclusion

Bioethics is strengthened by its interdisciplinary nature. The perspectives of law and medicine and philosophy and theology all contribute to a more complete understanding of the values in health care. The tensions among the perspectives certainly can lead to an unproductive animosity, but they can also lead to a greater clarity of thought. While drawing strong boundaries between and among the disciplines of bioethics would eviscerate this body of thought, blurring all distinctions presents its own disadvantages.

References

Alpers, Ann. "Criminal Act or Palliative Care?: Prosecutions Involving the Care of the Dying." *Journal of Law, Medicine & Ethics* 26 (1998): 308–331.

American Pain Society and American Academy of Pain Management. *The Use of Opioids for the Treatment of Chronic Pain* (1997).

Federation of State Medical Boards. *Model Guidelines for the Use of Controlled Substances for the Treatment of Pain* (1998).

Johnson, Sandra H. "End-of-Life Decision Making: What We Don't Know, We Make Up; What We Do Know, We Ignore." *Indiana Law Review* 31 (1998): 13–48.

Johnson, Sandra H., ed. "Symposium on Legal and Regulatory Issues in Pain Management." *Journal of Law, Medicine & Ethics* 24 (1996): 290–364.

Johnson, Sandra H., ed. "Symposium on Legal and Regulatory Issues in Pain Management." *Journal of Law, Medicine & Ethics* 26 (1998): 265–352.

Martino, Ann M. "In Search of a New Ethic for Treating Patients with Chronic Pain: What Can Medical Boards Do?" *Journal of Law, Medicine & Ethics* 26 (1998): 332–349.

SUPPORT Principal Investigators. "A Controlled Trial to Improve Care for Seriously Ill Hospitalized Patients: The Study to Understand Prognoses and Preferences for Outcomes and Risks of Treatment (SUPPORT)." *Journal of the American Medical Association* 274, no. 20 (1995): 1591–1598.

ETHICS IN HEALTH SCIENCES EDUCATION

Gerard Magill
Center for Health Care Ethics

INTRODUCTION

"What's ethics got to do with it?"—that is, with education in the health sciences? The Center for Health Care Ethics has a Ph.D. program that focuses upon ethics in health care. However, the purpose of this essay is to discuss the role of ethics in the other programs at Saint Louis University's Health Sciences Center. My purpose is to discuss ethics across the curriculum in graduate and professional programs in the health sciences, including the School of Medicine, the School of Nursing, the School of Public Health, and the Center for Advanced Dental Education. The Center for Health Care Ethics also has responsibility for many lectures, seminars, and tutorials both in formal settings (e.g., the *Research Ethics* course or our summer *Institutes*) and informal settings (e.g., our *Ethics for Lunch Series*). And the center publishes a monthly essay and a quarterly journal (*Health Care Ethics USA*) for faculty, staff, and students in the health sciences. This is a brief list of *what* the center does.

But *why* does the center bother?—that is the point raised by the question, *"What's ethics got to do with it?"* The reply to this question applies as much to the center's Ph.D. program in health care ethics as it does to the courses, lectures, seminars, and tutorials that the center offers in the health sciences. Our answer to the question *"What's ethics got to do with it?"* is in a sense very straightforward—basic ethical values are at the heart of fine education in the following sense. These basic values form our personal character and social fabric. These basic values shape our decision making processes that enable us to resolve ethical dilemmas and foster the good. And these basic values inspire right behavior that nourishes professional life and social interaction.

Hence, this essay discusses the crucial contribution of these basic values to education, especially in the Jesuit, Catholic tradition of Saint Louis University. By imbuing education with these basic values, our university inspires the finest scholarship and trains visionary leaders for

13

society. So ethics across the curriculum fosters excellence in education and also provides a stream of transformative leaders for society who seek common ground across specialties and even religious belief.[1]

A commitment to ethics across the curriculum highlights both the individual and the community we form in our education processes. And the cultivation of the reciprocal relation between the individual and the community is crucial to developing ethical sensitivities in the health sciences—after all, the health of the individual and the health of the community are inseparably connected.[2]

A Community of Scholars

To explore one approach to ethics across the curriculum I would like to play with some metaphors. Let us imagine ourselves in the Serengeti in Tanzania. The sun is slipping in the sky, and as the ripples of sight in the diminishing heat haze merge into clearer vision, under the dust cloud surrounding the watering hole appears a spectacular variety of God's creatures: some trundling, others scurrying, and a few soaring, but all seeking sustenance, including ourselves. Let us quench our thirst around this refreshing spring that we know as university life. But as we sip together we need to be attentive to reality, being wary of rustling shadows in the surrounding bush or the puzzling shapes in the water: lions and alligators sip and sup at watering holes!

I would like to splash you with some ideas, recognizing that my discourse only skims the surface of our deeper pool. My presentation on ethics across the curriculum from the perspective of health care focuses upon the relation between values and scholarship in the interdisciplinary context of graduate and professional education. This approach to ethics reflects the clinical and community experiences of the health sciences, but also pertains to graduate and professional education in general.

I begin with concerns that are increasingly prevalent in university life today. To address these concerns I consider how the mission of Jesuit education can help us to relate values and scholarship in graduate and professional education. My hope is to advance the discussion on "Ethics Across the Curriculum," suggesting tangible content and coherent meaning to claims about basic values in education.

One thing is for sure. As globalization extends into the new millennium, we will need to accommodate more and more creatures around our watering hole while also protecting its ecological fragility as an indispensable source of communal sustenance.

Concerns About Graduate and Professional Education

A cursory glance at almost any issue of *The Chronicle of Higher Education* rehearses many of the concerns in graduate education today. These concerns depict what Jaraslov Pelikan calls "a university in crisis" referring to "a crisis of confidence that is at the same time a crisis of self-confidence" and a "crisis of credibility."[3] There is an abundance of literature on this apparent crisis in university life.[4] These concerns generally can be related to three categories: personal, institutional, or social.

First, we read regularly of personal concerns, for example, the debt graduate students incur, or the difficulty in selecting a thesis or dissertation topic, or the length of professional and research programs. Moreover, sometimes there can be an impression among students that the academy is interested primarily in the welfare of the faculty rather than the students[5]—raising the thorny question of whether students are customers in the business of education.[6] Clinical and community health students are no exception to these concerns.

Second, we often encounter concerns in graduate and professional education that deal with institutional or organizational matters, for example, inadequate mentoring in course work and thesis or dissertation writing, or the jeopardy and career disruption that students face when graduate programs shrink or disappear. It is no surprise to encounter in *The Chronicle of Higher Education* a front-page item on the fall-out after cutting doctoral programs.[7] And the current environment of health care increasingly threatens education, especially in clinical programs, at our nation's schools in the health sciences.

Third, there is a plethora of social concerns that can consume graduate students. Graduate students encounter a social environment where workforce requirements mean that multiple careers increasingly will become a standard expectation and that academic positions may have to traverse the high wire without the perceived safety net of tenure.[8] The volatile nature of health care today exacerbates this problem of career stability for graduates in the health sciences.

Fortunately, we are not bereft of resources to alleviate these concerns. There are distinctive characteristics of Jesuit education that provide assistance, inspiring the values that can permeate a program for ethics across the curriculum. My presentation traces three basic values in the Jesuit mission of education that are crucial to any program for ethics across the curriculum.

I intentionally address these basic values in language amenable to leadership development in the health sciences: the values of independence, interdependence, and influence. However, these values explicitly reflect foundational insights in the Catholic tradition of ethics. First, the value of *independence* reflects the dignity and sanctity of the human person whose autonomy is a central focus for health care professionals. Second, the value of *interdependence* reflects the common good that fosters a sense of mutuality and connectedness among careers and cared-for in health care. Third, the value of *influence* reflects the preferential option for the poor and suffering that continually urges health care to seek policy reforms. Before examining these basic values, it is helpful to see how they emerge from the Jesuit mission in education.

The Jesuit Mission

In our university's mission there are three distinctive characteristics of Jesuit education. The first characteristic emphasizes spirituality, which has become better defined as "the spiritual humanism of the Jesuits."[9] This phrase captures the core of our university's mission, which is the "pursuit of truth for the greater glory of God and service of humanity . . . guided by the spiritual and intellectual ideals of the Society of Jesus."[10] While spiritual humanism necessarily includes a community dimension, it also draws attention to the dignity and sanctity of each individual. Hence, spiritual humanism, as distinctive of Jesuit education, inspires the value of *independence* in graduate study.

The other two hallmarks of our Jesuit mission are holistic education and social transformation. These two characteristics inspire *interdependence* and *influence* in turn. Spiritual humanism urges social transformation in the sense of fostering a call "to transform society in the spirit of the Gospels" as indicated in our university's mission statement.[11] This call involves being "effective leaders of social change"[12] and developing "lifelong habits of service to others."[13] Hence, social transformation, as distinctive of Jesuit education, inspires the value of influence in graduate study.

The three values of *independence, interdependence,* and *influence* are especially important for clinical and community health arenas. The paradigms of allowing one of these values to trump the others (for example, medical education's focus upon patient autonomy) have fortunately gone by the way.[14]

Values and Scholarship

Jesuit education inspires three crucial values that can address the concerns of our students and provide beacons of light for scholarship in graduate study. These values address personal concerns in terms of the value of *independence*, institutional concerns in terms of the value of *interdependence*, and social concerns in terms of the value of *influence* that engages university and society.

My analysis of these three basic values adopts a twofold hermeneutic. On the one hand, these basic values integrate experience, reflection, and action. On the other hand, these basic values explicitly develop the Catholic tradition's respect for human dignity, the common good, and the preferential option for the poor.

I develop my analysis by explicitly associating these three basic values with what can be called "value traits" or characteristics. These three values bind us together in a scholarly community that assists one another to become excellent leaders in our shared quest for truth in society.

In clinical and community health education it is crucial to foster a sensitivity to foundational values that permeate professional life and to avoid approaches to specialties that truncate the necessary connections between the professions—we may be quite different animals, but we need to work well together for the interests of all. The values that I now want to discuss exhort us to be peaceable with one another as we sip together at the watering hole.

INDEPENDENCE

When faculty empower graduate students to develop critical thinking there is a shift from dependence to independence.[15] If we can assume that independence associated with critical inquiry is indispensable for graduate education, other value traits can be identified as conducive to graduate scholarship.

Self-Awareness

In an age of globalization, self-awareness based on concrete experiences and differences enables communities to retain their identity and legitimacy. Similarly, enhancing self-awareness in self-respect and personal dignity is indispensable in graduate education. Of course, gender will continue to be a dominant category here for some time.[16] Self-awareness honors the injunction of Socrates, "know thyself," and is crucial for what Daniel Goleman refers to as "emotional intelligence."[17]   Moreover, self-awareness breeds a self-confidence that resists paternalism and authoritarianism, which notoriously stifle ingenuity in scholarship. Above all, self-awareness leads to belief in self that facilitates discerning which area of scholarship students should select. Before we dream of careers, we really need to know who we are. Hence, the personal value trait of self-awareness provides an ongoing resource for successful scholarship in graduate education.

Foresight

To explain the value of foresight, perhaps another metaphor can help. If self-awareness provides the fuel for graduate education, then foresight provides the road-map. Of all the questions worth asking in graduate education, perhaps the most important is "why"? By responding to this question students establish an academic mission for themselves that should direct all subsequent decisions in their graduate programs. This mission spawns the hope that helps them to build their academic careers. Being able to anticipate the outcome of graduate education can be a helpful condition for achieving success therein, and, I would suggest somewhat controversially, the more proactive students are, the more they design the trajectory of their education, the more successful that experience will be. To elaborate on this controversial point, I suggest that graduate students should consider their courses, their thesis and dissertations, and their expected career options in an integrated fashion that invests in staged development. How can students nurture foresight? First, mentoring by faculty is crucial—after all, faculty with foresight tend to be the best teachers. Second, foresight requires relating the head and the heart, reason and sentiment, as students anticipate their academic futures: the heart has reasons that the head does not know.

Commitment

To adopt a travel metaphor, if self-awareness provides the fuel for graduate education and foresight the road-map, then commitment leads us forward on the journey. Commitment enables the student to traverse the program by establishing priorities and accomplishing goals. Commitment requires students to address their personal circumstances both honestly and courageously. Perseverance is implied by commitment, but only in the sense of responding with integrity to variations in circumstances. Interestingly, commitment does not mean sticking it out in a given program, no matter what.

Conclusion

In sum, ethics across the curriculum highlights the value of independence, which enhances scholarship in graduate and professional education by weaving together the value traits of self-awareness, foresight, and commitment. Together, these value traits generate among graduate students a sense of identity and optimism without which personal happiness and professional success will flounder. In particular, the integration of self-awareness, foresight, and commitment enables professionals in clinical and community health to foster their autonomy and competence, but always in service to others.[18]

When we sip at the watering hole, we can imbibe the spring water only as individuals, independently. But we can take comfort that as other individuals in the herd sip with us, our flanks are protected.

The types of competencies that can be aligned with the value of independence and its congruent value traits cluster around the techniques each individual student needs to learn for gathering data: I am sure you recall the old chestnut, *"Trust in God: all others bring data!"* These competencies include: skills for critical inquiry and inference, especially with regard to analysis, hypothesis, and verification; hermeneutics and research methods, for example, qualitative and quantitative research methodology; and using library research resources and the role of primary and secondary literature in scholarship. Moreover, this value can be related very well to the professional principles of integrity, honesty, etc.

There may appear to be a *prima facie* contradiction between the values of independence and interdependence in scholarship. Of course, there is no contradiction. After all, what sports team could be successful without athletes who excel as individuals? In reality, then, students need to develop both values in order to flourish if sound scholarship is to prevail.

INTERDEPENDENCE

To ascertain what the value of interdependence[19] contributes to graduate education, I deploy the same strategy as previously.

Collaboration

If it is true that globalization can be counterbalanced by a process of self-awareness, it is also true that cultural units across the globe can survive by developing collaborative relations that are mutually beneficial. Analogously, graduate students with critical self-awareness can flourish by collaboration in an array of networks that enhance their education. Mastering the techniques of teamwork presents endless opportunities for advancing their scholarship. This value trait combines belief in self, characteristic of being independent, with an interdependent belief in others.

Collaboration unveils an abundance of resources that pertain only to situations where individuals, who are not necessarily like-minded, cooperate with professional empathy. When graduate programs empower students to work with and not against one another, not only can their research benefit by reaching further and seeing deeper, but those involved can become better people basking in their shared wisdom.

Integration

The value trait of integration spurs students to coordinate the multi-disciplinary aspects of graduate education. If students want to fulfill the reasons *why* they enter graduate programs, they require more than meeting their curricular and career needs. The common enterprise that students share and shape invites them to marshal available resources within their department and across disciplinary lines. This sharing instigates hope in building a community of scholars whose synergy helps them to pursue their own research agendas and thereby realize their academic goals. Of the clichés about university life, Jaraslov Pelikan insists there is none more worth keeping than the "community of scholars."[20]

Integrating resources requires a mentoring process by experienced faculty throughout the academic program. Otherwise, students can be in jeopardy of relegating their research to the narrow confines of isolated or idiosyncratic pursuits. But if their imaginations perceive connections with other fields and disciplines, they can spark a creativity that enhances the interpretative depth of their work while contributing to the multidisciplinary enterprise of graduate education.

Dedication

The value trait of dedication allows students to honor the collaborative and integrative environment of their education as they apply themselves vigorously to their work. We should attribute the dedication of students to scholarship as a commitment not merely to their own research but also to their learning environment. That is, students ought to engage their learning environment generously, upholding and promoting it in the dynamic reciprocity of interdependent, scholarly discourse.

Conclusion

In sum, ethics across the curriculum highlights the value of interdependence which enhances scholarship in graduate education by weaving together the value traits of collaboration, integration, and dedication. Together, these value traits generate among graduate students a sense of holistic education that encourages them to be imaginative as they pursue their studies within a community of scholars. In particular, the integration of collaboration, integration, and dedication enables professionals in clinical and community health to foster a team-oriented spirit that locates needs and resources of individuals within community contexts,[21] some being religiously inspired.[22]

Hence, the value of interdependence allows us to replace the "sink or swim" approach to academic life. As we sip together at our watering hole we can assist one another cooperatively, perhaps showing the recently arrived the safer shallows, or preventing the incautious from wading too deep, or enticing the more advanced to swim out in the wake of the experienced.

The types of competencies that can be aligned with the value of interdependence and its congruent value traits cluster around the techniques that students need for collaborative endeavors. These skills include: decision making and assessment processes; research protocols (for example, regarding human subjects); writing and teaching techniques; languages and technological literacy, especially with regard to databases and the inter/intranet; and, not least, competencies for colloquia, conferences, and publication. It seems indispensable to associate with interdependence competencies for effective communication in good writing, fine teaching, and persuasive discourse. Moreover, principles of consent and confidentiality obviously relate to this value of interdependence.

The value of interdependence in graduate education is the bedrock for interdisciplinary scholarship. By fostering a community of scholars who engage one another across disciplines, we establish a learning environment that benefits the critical inquiry within disciplines by discourse among them. I have suggested previously that scholarship within each discipline flourishes when we imbue graduate education with the value of dependence and its congruent value traits of self-awareness, foresight, and commitment. Here, I am suggesting that interdisciplinary scholarship flourishes when we imbue graduate education with the value of interdependence and its congruent value traits of collaboration, integration, and dedication. That is, self-awareness enables us to be aware of others in a way that facilitates collaboration; foresight provides us with an academic mission that provokes integration of personnel and resources as we pursue our goals; and commitment applies our energies to study, thereby inspiring a dedication to academic life that enhances our learning environment.

However, the relation between values and scholarship in graduate education needs to be expanded further still. The confluence of dependence and interdependence as two distinct currents at our watering hole meet in a mainstream that flows into the public realm: I refer to this mainstream as the value of influence upon our society.

INFLUENCE

The value of influence deals with the interaction between graduate education and the public realm.[23] Jaraslov Pelikan relates the "crisis of the university" to the "crises of the age beyond its walls."[24] Likewise, David O'Brien argues from a religious perspective for the university to find its center outside itself.[25] If our values can address our concerns within the university, the same values can assist the crises beyond its walls.[26]

The confluence of dependence and independence in graduate education can dynamically engage the social transformation of our culture, including religion and society alike.[27] To understand the significance of this value of influence I will delineate its congruent value traits and explain how they coalesce with the value traits in my previous analysis.

Conscientization

Conscientization has emerged as a process that can safeguard communities and cultures against the excesses of globalization in our postmodern world. Likewise, by becoming more aware of our own society we can enhance its culture through the abundant and varied discourse of graduate education. Jaraslov Pelikan has observed that "one of the most besetting vices of the university . . . has always been its quaint tendency to look inward and ignore the context of society within which it exists and without which it could not exist."[28] Students cannot properly have awareness of self (which I align with the value of independence) or collaboration with others within the university (which

I align with the value of interdependence) without also cultivating critical consciousness about society and culture (which I align with the value of influence).

Critical awareness of society can enhance belief in it. In other words, the belief we have in ourselves and in our colleagues within the university must not be detached from our belief in society. To disassociate any one from the others would result in a truncated identity of who we are as scholars in a complex world. However, we will be wise to heed Samuel Huntington's warning in his book, *The Clash of Civilizations*, about avoiding the extreme of reducing meaning and identity to cultural commonality.[29]

Reconciliation

Graduate education can engage society effectively when it coordinates its resources to replace social fragmentation with appropriate reconciliation. The value trait of reconciliation attempts, by anticipating opportunities for participative collaboration, to harness the legitimate diversities that all too often assert themselves in conflict rather than cooperation. Students cannot properly have foresight about their academic mission (which I align with the value of independence) or integrate the academic resources available to achieve their scholarly goal (which I align with the value of interdependence) without also cultivating their responsibility for social reconciliation (which I align with the value of influence). The hope that students foster with regard to building their academic careers within the community of scholars at the university naturally culminates in the hope that builds cultural cohesion in the public realm.

Mentoring necessarily plays a crucial role in nurturing the value trait of reconciliation, especially by faculty whose academic work manifestly advocates for social transformation. And we must anticipate opportunities for relating graduate education with social transformation, developing our imagination as a repository of social wisdom that transcends the strictures of individual talent.

Advocacy

When we avail ourselves of these opportunities, we give witness to the service that academic life and graduate education can offer to society. The value trait of advocacy engages us in the practice of relating academic life to discourse in the public realm. This practice has not always characterized Catholic higher education as Philip Gleason reminds us,[30] for example, when the practice is construed as secularizing Catholic education.[31] However, Jaraslov Pelikan has remarked, perhaps with some rhetorical exaggeration, that duties to society have legitimate claims upon universities as "the greatest and most important centers in modern times for cultural and national life."[32] Hence, students cannot properly have a commitment to study (which I align with the value of independence) or have a dedication to academic life that enhances their learning environment (which I align with the value of interdependence) without also developing their advocacy for social transformation (which I align with the value of influence). Advocacy, then, demands that we engage university life with public service generously, at least in the sense of contributing to social and cultural discourse.

However, this value trait of advocacy is double-edged insofar as it refers to the shift from theory to practice that is so indispensable in contemporary hermeneutical thought. Therefore, as we consider the influence of university education upon social transformation, hermeneutically the process necessarily entails a reciprocal influence. It behooves us to acknowledge the practical influence that social transformation can have upon university education.

Conclusion

In sum, ethics across the curriculum highlights the value of influence which enhances scholarship in graduate education by weaving together the value traits of conscientization, reconciliation, and advocacy. Together, these value traits generate among graduate students a sense of social responsibility that dynamically engages their education with the public realm.[33] In particular, the integration of conscientization, reconciliation, and advocacy enables professionals in clinical and community health to foster a sensitivity (often religiously grounded) to the needs of the marginalized in the community who can be overlooked by health and social services.[34]

So, as we sip together at the watering hole, we needn't be surprised to see more than our own herd refreshing themselves. In fact, we should hope to be surrounded by creatures different from ourselves. And by looking around we can determine the sort of creature we are—after all, we have a way to go before the lion and the lamb sip together!

The types of competencies that can be aligned with the value of influence and its congruent value traits cluster around the techniques that students need for being citizen scholars, demanding daily sweat and tedious toil, in contrast to the leisurely ways of the proverbial gentleman scholar. Oh that scholarship could be that easy! These competencies for discourse in the public realm include: skills in creating partnerships that solicit grants and foundation support; skills in democratic processes that promote solidarity, subsidiarity, and justice; leadership and lobbying skills that engage policy concerns, at least with regard to the educational enterprise.

GENERAL CONCLUSION

Diane Ravitch argues in her book, *The Schools We Deserve*, that we must take responsibility for the educational crisis in our times.[35] I have presented an argument to address the concerns that fuel this apparent crisis in university life by discussing an approach to ethics across the curriculum. We can nurture values (inspired by the distinctive mission of Jesuit education) that enhance scholarship and enable us to float interdisciplinary suggestions for our Jesuit mission that develop its educational identity as we move into the next millennium. In graduate education in the health sciences the values of *independence*, *interdependence*, and *influence* provide a superb foundation for professional life. The value of *independence* reminds clinical and community health practitioners that professional competence and patient autonomy are indispensable. But the value of *interdependence* emphasizes that our professional competencies intermingle in a manner that requires us to work collaboratively for the sake of the greater good in the community. And the value of *influence* urges us to turn our professionalism to advocate for the needy, the marginalized, and the deprived in society—for if we do not, who can?

These three values are inspired by what is distinctive in Jesuit education—and they enable us to recognize spiritual humanism and holistic education as converging currents that sweep graduate education into the mainstream of social transformation.

I have described three basic values in language amenable to leadership development in the health sciences: *independence*, *interdependence*, and *influence*. These values explicitly reflect foundational insights in the Catholic tradition of ethics, as follows. First, the value of *independence* reflects the dignity and sanctity of the human person whose autonomy is a central focus for health care professionals. Second, the value of *interdependence* reflects the common good that fosters a sense of mutuality and connectedness among careers and cared-for in health care. Third, the value of *influence* reflects the preferential option for the poor and suffering that continually urges health care to seek policy reforms.

Well, the sun has gone down now in the Serengeti and many of our visitors, sufficiently refreshed, have departed from the watering hole into the quiet night: some to rest, others to explore what Mother Nature has to offer. We too can slip away for a while, perhaps more attentive to the ecological fragility of our watering-hole and maybe more confident in its replenishing abundance as an indispensable source of communal sustenance. As a gathering place for our program on ethics across the curriculum, like our creature friends let us be wary of those rustling shadows in the surrounding bush.

Notes

[1] See, for example, Vincent Kiernan, "Can Science and Theology Find Common Ground?" *The Chronicle of Higher Education* (30 April 1999): A17–A19.

[2] See Benjamin C. Amick et al., eds., *Society & Health* (New York: Oxford University Press, 1995), v–x.

[3] Jaraslov Pelikan, *The Idea of a University: A Reexamination* (New Haven: Yale University Press, 1992), 12, 21.

[4] As evidenced, for example, in the widespread and sympathetic response to Allan Bloom's book, *The Closing of the American Mind*, on the failure of higher education. Allan Bloom, *The Closing of the American Mind: How Higher Education Has Failed Democracy and Impoverished the Souls of Today's Students* (New York: Simon and Schuster, 1987). For other references, see Pelikan, 191; Charles J. Sykes, *Profscam: Professors and the Demise of Higher Education* (Washington, DC: Regenery Gateway, 1988) on allegations of financial and ethical corruption among professors; Roger Kimball, *Tenured Radicals: How Politics Has Corrupted Our Higher Education* (New York: Harper and Row, 1990) on a new political orthodoxy of the Left in university departments of literature and the humanities; Dinesh D'Souza, *Illiberal Education: The Politics of Race and Sex on Campus* (New York: Free Press, 1991); Page Smith, *Killing the Spirit: Higher Education in America* (New York: Penguin Books, 1991) on betrayal in the history of higher education in America; Bruce Wilshire, *The Moral Collapse of the University* (Albany: State University of New York Press, 1990) on the inability of the university to form and express a sense of conscience.

[5] See, for example, Thomas Sowell, "Titanic Problems in Academe," *Forbes* (30 November 1998): 82.

[6] See, for example, Robert Letovsky, "Are Our Students Our Customers?" *Leadership Connection* (spring 1998): 1.

[7] Robin Wilson, "When Doctoral Programs Are Eliminated, Everybody Faces Difficult Choices," *The Chronicle of Higher Education* (18 October 1996): A1, A10–11. Also see, Denise K. Magner, "Master's Degrees Are the Hot Topic at a Meeting on Doctoral Education," *The Chronicle of Higher Education* (30 April 1999): A16.

[8] Courtney Leatherman, "More Faculty Members Question the Value of Tenure," *The Chronicle of Higher Education* (25 October 1996): A12–13.

[9] Ronald Modras, "The Spiritual Humanism of the Jesuits," *America* (4 February 1995): 10–18.

[10] "Saint Louis University Mission Statement," see *Strategic Plan*, 1. The role of spiritual humanism in Jesuit education is evident in our university's *Strategic Plan*: "A

Saint Louis University education is faith-centered and seeks to increase every student's spiritual awareness and personal religious commitment" (*Strategic Plan*, iii).

[11] "University Mission Statement," *Strategic Plan*, 1.

[12] "President Biondi's Vision for Saint Louis University," *Strategic Plan*, 1.

[13] *Strategic Plan*, iii.

[14] See John D. Arras and Bonnie Steinbock, "Foundations of the Health Professional-Patient Relationship," pt. 1 of *Ethical Issues in Modern Medicine,* 5th ed. (Toronto: Mayfield, 1999), 41–50; and Kevin O'Rourke and Benedict Ashley, "The Healing Professions: Response of the Community to the Health Needs of Persons," pt. 2 of *Health Care Ethics*, 4th ed. (Washington, DC: Georgetown University Press, 1997), 67–136.

[15] For an explanation of these values, see Peter Senge's emphasis upon "personal mastery" and "mental models" in his approach to continuous learning. See Peter Senge, et al., *The Fifth Discipline Fieldbook: Strategies and Tools for Building a Learning Organization* (New York: Doubleday, 1994) on "personal mastery" (pp. 193–232) and on "mental models" (pp. 235–293).

[16] For example, Frank Crouch, "Gender Parity Improves in Religion and Theology Doctorates; Still Lags Behind Other Humanities," *The Chronicle of Higher Education*, 11, no. 4 (November 1996): 1. In 1994, of the combined doctorates in religion and theology, 79% were men and 21% women, in contrast to the humanities where 52% were men and 48% women.

[17] Daniel Goleman, *Emotional Intelligence* (London: Bloomsbury, 1996), 43, referring to Socrates, 46. Here he follows Gardner's proposal for emotional intelligence. Howard Gardner, *Multiple Intelligences: The Theory in Practice* (New York: Basic Books, 1993).

[18] For example, Lawrence David Weiss, *Private Medicine and Public Health* (Boulder CO: Westview Press, 1997).

[19] See Peter Senge et al., *The Fifth Discipline Fieldbook*, on "shared vision" (pp. 297–346) and on "team learning" (pp. 351–440).

[20] Pelikan, *The Idea of a University*, 57.

[21] Edmund Pellegrino and David Thomasma, *The Virtues in Medical Practice* (New York: Oxford University Press, 1993), especially chapter 2.

[22] Edmund Pellegrino and David Thomasma, *Helping and Healing: Religious Commitment in Health Care* (Washington, DC: Georgetown University Press, 1997).

[23] See Peter Senge et al., *The Fifth Discipline Fieldbook* on "systems thinking" (pp. 87–189).

[24] Pelikan, *The Idea of the University*, 13.

[25] David J. O'Brien, *From the Heart of the American Church: Catholic Higher Education and American Culture* (Maryknoll, New York: Orbis Books, 1994), 190, referring to a presentation by the theologian Jon Sobrino.

[26] The U.S. bishops exhort Catholic higher education to provide society with leadership in matters of justice and human rights in particular. U.S. Bishops Pastoral Letter, *Catholic Higher Education and the Pastoral Mission of the Church* (Washington DC: USCC, 1980), par. 10, cited in O'Brien, *From the Heart of the American Church*, 189.

[27] In a sense, here I am relating together two of David Tracy's well-known three publics, the church and society—his other public being the academy. On the role of an *arguing* community of inquiry and a *conversing* community of interpretation in these public domains, see these works: David Tracy, *The Analogical Imagination: Christian Theology and the Culture of Pluralism* (New York: Crossroads, 1981), 449–453; and

David Tracy, *Plurality and Ambiguity: Hermeneutics, Religion, and Hope* (San Francisco: Harper & Row, 1987), 1–27.

[28] Pelikan, *The Idea of a University*, 137.

[29] Samuel P. Huntington, *The Clash of Civilization and the Remaking of World Order* (Simon & Schuster, 1996). "Peoples and countries with different cultures are coming apart. Alignments defined by ideology and superpower relations are giving way to alignments defined by culture and civilization." *New York Times* (6 November 1996): B2.

[30] Philip Gleason, "American Catholic Higher Education: A Historical Perspective," in *The Shape of Catholic Higher Education*, ed. Robert Hassenger (Chicago, 1967), 15–53, cited in O'Brien, *From the Heart of the American Church*, 218, n.7.

[31] See, William Leahy, S.J., *Adapting to America: Catholics, Jesuits, and Higher Education in the Twentieth Century* (Washington, DC: 1991), 100, referring to a group of lay faculty at St. John's University, New York, in 1967, who denounced separate incorporation based on this argument (cited by O'Brien, 223, n.2).

[32] Pelikan, *The Idea of a University*, 139.

[33] For example, Audrey Chapman, ed. *Health Care Reform: A Human Rights Approach* (Washington, DC: Georgetown University Press, 1994).

[34] See, for example, Stanley W. Carlson-Thies and James W. Skillen, ed. *Welfare in America: Christian Perspectives on a Policy in Crisis* (Grand Rapids, MI: Eerdmans, 1996), especially section II.

[35] Diane Ravitch, *The Schools We Deserve: Reflections on the Educational Crisis of Our Times* (New York: Basic Books, 1985).

MAKING CHOICES: TEACHING BUSINESS ETHICS

James E. Fisher
Emerson Electric Center for Business Ethics

Introduction

Case studies are a mainstay in many business schools and courses. These narratives typically relate actual business situations, with the best of them engaging a student's imagination, inviting that student to step into the role of business manager, to sift through information that is inevitably incomplete and often ambiguous, and then to decide. In this way, case studies simulate the tasks of business managers, namely, to make choices that are themselves only partially understood, and to make these choices while constrained by pressures of time and money.

The best managers embrace this reality and have not only the competence but also the confidence and courage to make good choices. This truth, of course, extends to the ethical decisions that managers must make, and business schools have a significant responsibility to prepare their students for this reality.

In the Classroom: A Case Example

One case[1] that I commonly use in both marketing and business ethics classes relates a situation in which a young man receives an unexpected promotion, becoming a sales representative with a plum territorial assignment for a firm that manufactures and sells children's clothing. We are informed that the sales manager is out of the country and, therefore, the newly appointed sales representative must introduce himself to important customers in the territory. The case outlines a planned dinner meeting between the salesman and a buyer representing a large department store chain. The case apparently ends at this point and students will pick up various threads of discussion, all typically related to personal selling and its attendant challenges of establishing customer relationships, managing time, and meeting company expectations.

The case continues, however, with a supplement[2] handed out in class that relates the substance of the dinner meeting between our young salesman and his department store customer, a shrewd buyer with over 20 years of retailing experience. The buyer explains that the previous sales representative (now deceased) had taken "special care of my needs" in the form of "a little bonus" paid at the beginning of each major season. "I didn't know that," is all our young salesman can muster in the way of a reply. The buyer expresses his hope that they too can "work together" in this way, but in so doing also makes a veiled threat to shift his business to competitors. The case concludes observing that an "uneasy silence ensued."

I place my students in the midst of this uneasy silence and ask them how they intend to break it: "What will you say to the buyer?" While student responses are frequently thoughtful, they usually lack decisiveness. Most seek to stall, to delay, or otherwise dissemble. Some want managerial advice and direction. Others believe that further information will clarify the situation, hopeful that some paper trail or an artfully framed question will yield the necessary insight. Not infrequently, a feckless student will inevitably propose paying the "bonus," observing that the payment is small and the business (and commission) large.

The scenario presented in this case is not a highly nuanced one; no exquisite dilemma here with right versus right or conflicting responsibilities. The buyer is soliciting a bribe and the salesman should not pay it. To do so would be illegal, unethical, and imprudent. And yet, I believe that the case provides the class with a rich experience along several dimensions. It gives the students a realistic sense of how ethical choices often arise in a business context. A young professional, long on ambition and short on experience, prepares for business-as-usual, but then faces an unexpected choice that is all the more disorienting for its immediacy. The ethics of business is a muscular one, demanding a real-time response, a decisive word to break an ambiguous silence.

There is then the pragmatic issue in this case of just how one goes about saying "no" to the buyer. Is the suggestion curtly brushed aside? Should alternative (legal) arrangements be considered? Would humor possibly defuse a difficult situation? This is a fertile vein to mine in the teaching of business ethics. Peter Drucker's distinction between doing the right thing and doing things right seems relevant here as future managers are challenged to think about how precisely one goes about implementing ethical choices in effective ways.

Business Ethics: The Issues

Any attempt to catalogue the issues relevant to business ethics must seriously consider the question of perspective. Business schools, insofar as they are engaged in pre-professional and professional education, are instrumental in developing among their students an understanding and appreciation for the role responsibilities of business professionals. At the same time, this educational process invites an examination and assessment of one's own values and priorities. In particular, the prospect of role conflict emerges as students appreciate the very specific and important responsibilities that economic agents assume and how the integration of these responsibilities with other legitimate ones is often difficult and uncertain.[3]

It is also useful for students taking up business ethics issues to consider the role of business organizations in a broader economic, social, and historical context. Even with the ascendance of capitalism and the globalization of economic systems—or precisely because of these trends—it is important for potential business professionals to recognize that the distinctive relationships among business, government, and other stakeholders remain dynamic issues with significant moral and managerial implications. Legal and cultural norms still vary across nations and regions and this variance presents important challenges for business conduct as well as a valuable opportunity to raise important questions about the role of capital and labor, distributional equity, and the nature of the social contract.

Somewhere between these individual and societal perspectives is the organizational view, which takes up the complex responsibilities facing managers who must in some sense balance the interests and rights of owners, employees, customers, and other stakeholders. Leadership and the moral responsibilities of organizational leaders are often examined in this context. These issues are frequently the ones that dominate discussions of business ethics. One taxonomy of these issues, summarized in Table 1, identifies four ethical categories. Some 27 problems[4] are placed into the four categories of equity, rights, honesty, and the exercise of corporate power.

Table 1:
Ethical Categories of Corporate Issues

Equity	Rights	Honesty	Exercise of Corporate Power
Executive Salaries	Corporate Due Process	Employee Conflicts of Interest	Political Action Committees
Comparable Worth	Employee Health Screening	Security of Company Records	Workplace Safety
Product Pricing	Employee Privacy	Inappropriate Gifts	Product Safety
	Sexual Harassment	Unauthorized Payment to Foreign Officials	Environmental Issues
	Affirmative Action & Equal Employment Opportunity	Advertising Content	Disinvestment
	Shareholder Interests	Government Contract Issues	Corporate Contributions
	Employment at Will	Financial and Cash Management Procedures	Social Issues Raised by Religious Organizations
	Whistle Blowing	Conflicts Between the Corporation's Ethical System and Accepted Business Practices in Foreign Countries	Plant/Facility Closures and Downsizing

Source: The Conference Board's *Corporate Ethics*, Research Report No. 900, 1988.

There is at least one more perspective that may be of special relevance for those teaching business ethics. It is a perspective described by Badaracco and Webb[5] as a "view from the trenches" and is based on in-depth interviews with young business professionals. Their findings suggest that the experience of young managers in the workplace is one in which performance pressures and the demand to be a team player frequently crowd out ethical sensibilities. While illegal activities are clearly proscribed, the limits are often tested to the point that many of the interviewees report implicit and explicit pressures to do things "sleazy," if not exactly illegal. Not surprisingly, corporate ethics programs are perceived to be largely ineffectual, with weak enforcement and uncertain discipline. As a result, these young managers feel little connection with either their immediate supervisors or top executives. When confronted with ethical choices, these individuals are likely to handle such matters with informal, subjective techniques. They "resolved the dilemmas they faced largely on the basis of personal reflection and individual values, not through reliance on corporate credos, company loyalty, the exhortation of senior executives, philosophical principle, or religious reflection."[6]

Many of these young professionals seem to place a premium on self-reliance and mobility as career paths are charted. Most are wary of over investment in corporate loyalty and organizational commitment. Thus for these individuals "being ethical involves fidelity to one's own values and a willingness to leave an organization that fails to match these values. . . . Ethics was a matter of exit, rather than loyalty or voice."[7] As experience is gained, many young managers take on a certain realism and mental toughness that can serve them well in their work, but for some the cumulative result can be isolation and even alienation. Here is one account:

> It was a wake-up call in a lot of ways. Definitely on how organizations work. You can get stranded alone. It showed me that you alone are responsible for yourself, for your professional and personal development. It gave me a bit of distance on people.[8]

Making Choices

Business ethics is about making choices. So too is the *teaching* of business ethics. Although the paired alternatives identified in Table 2 are not mutually exclusive, they do suggest that matters of emphasis will strongly influence the nature of our business ethics courses.

Table 2:
Making Choices: Contrasting Approaches in Teaching Business Ethics

Right Versus Right	Right Versus Wrong
Ethical Decision Making	Implementing Moral Choices
Conceptual	Pragmatic
Objective Morality	Personal Morality
Analytical Rigor	Professional Wisdom

It is sometimes said that there are two kinds of ethical problems: knowing what is right but not doing it and not knowing what is right. My impression is that efforts to teach business ethics have often tended to focus on the latter—moral dilemmas in which right versus right, where one apparently legitimate claim conflicts with another. The work of Badaracco and Webb would strongly suggest that issues of right versus wrong deserve more emphasis than they have typically received. This, in turn, would have implications for both the content and aim of business ethics courses.

There is little to suggest that abstract rules or principles currently motivate or inform the moral decision making of young managers. Utilitarian or deontological approaches often favored in business ethics courses need to be presented in a way that allows students to feel the weight of such moral theorizing in a more realistic and motivating way. Such approaches deserve time and attention and may offer an effective counterbalance to more subjective and personalized styles. Alternatively, Badaracco and Webb offer the suggestion that as teachers consider philosophical sources for business ethics, Aristotle and Machiavelli might "share the spotlight" with Mill and Kant.[9]

Ultimately out students will need the discipline and character that inform an active sense of professional responsibility.[10] The challenge they face is not only to make the right choices, but also to find feasible and effective ways to do the right thing in organizations that are themselves often highly charged political and competitive environments.

Notes

[1] Benson Shapiro, *Petite Playthings, Inc., 1984 (A)* (Boston, MA: HBS Publishing Service, 1984).

[2] Benson Shapiro, *Petite Playthings, Inc., 1984 (B)* (Boston, MA: HBS Publishing Service, 1984).

[3] This idea that the moral dilemmas of managers arise from conflicts among or within different spheres of responsibilities provides the analytic framework for Joseph L. Badaracco, Jr., *Business Ethics: Roles and Responsibilities* (Chicago: Richard D. Irwin, Inc., 1995). See also Michael Walzer, *Spheres of Justice* (New York: Basic Books, 1993).

[4] When surveyed, CEOs were most likely to identify the following as significant ethical issues for their businesses: employee conflicts of interest, inappropriate gifts to corporate personnel, sexual harassment, unauthorized payments, affirmative action, employee privacy, and environmental issues. Thus issues of rights and honesty were more likely to appear at the top of the list. See Ronald E. Berenbeim, *Corporate Ethics,* The Conference Board, 1988, Report No. 900, p. 3.

[5] Joseph L. Badaracco, Jr. and Allen P. Webb, "Business Ethics: A View from the Trenches," *California Management Review* 37, no. 2 (winter 1995): 8–28.

[6] *Ibid.*, 9.

[7] *Ibid.*, 21.

[8] *Ibid.*

[9] *Ibid.*, 25.

[10] For an excellent treatment of this topic, see Larry May, *The Socially Responsive Self: Social Theory and Professional Ethics* (Chicago: The University of Chicago Press, 1996).

WHAT HAS ETHICS GOT TO DO
WITH TEACHING LAW?

Dennis J. Tuchler
School of Law

Should the teaching of ethics be part of the training of a lawyer?[1] The answer given by most law faculties in the 1950s and 1960s was a simple "No."[2] Indeed, it would be unethical for a teacher to insert ethics into the lawyer's training. It would be unethical because it would be dishonest, and because it would violate the law teacher's duty to train the law student for the practice of law. It would be dishonest because it would give the student an unreal view of the legal system. It is a violation of the teacher's duty for that teacher to limit the ability of the student to practice law by making the student the teacher's instrument for social reform.

This approach to the teaching of law rests on a positivistic view of law and a view of our society as democratic and individualistic, emphasizing individual rights and leaving such concepts as right conduct, the public good, or the general welfare to the legislative branch of government. The lawyer's job is to understand how legal rules limit and direct conduct, and to advise clients accordingly. Ethics are not law, but are matters for individual choice based on subjective and contestable ideas of what is right and good. They are "subjective" in that they are understandable only by the person whose ethics they are, and they are contestable grounds for judgments by one person about the conduct of another simply because there can be found no general agreement as to what is right conduct. It is not the lawyer's job to judge the client or the client's aims, but rather it is to serve the client and to understand those aims and how to achieve them according to law. The lawyer's duty of loyalty to the client is done only by maximizing the client's individual liberty to pursue the latter's own ends in the context of the legal system. Moreover, the legal system itself is open to interpretation as a rule of law is applicable in the particular case of the client. Of course, the lawyer is assumed to have ethics that guide the lawyer's own life, and one of those ethics is the duty of loyalty to the client.[3] It is the lawyer's (ethical) duty to find the most efficient way through the law for the client in the pursuit of the client's selfish purposes. The lawyer violates that duty of loyalty by imposing the lawyer's own ethical standards on the client, letting those ethics shape and limit the service the lawyer gives the client.

Things have changed. The American Bar Association has decided that ethics is, indeed, an important part of the training of lawyers. Many law teachers, especially in elite law schools, agree. The question is no longer whether, but how, to teach legal ethics to law students, and what the content of that teaching should be. One part of the "how" question is answered by establishing a required course in professional responsibility which focuses on the rules governing lawyer conduct. Depending on time constraints, such a course might also go beyond those rules and consider questions of right and wrong conduct. Legal ethics might also be taught in other courses. It is left up to teachers of those courses to determine whether and how to deal with questions of professional responsibility.[4]

The other part of the "how" question has been answered by treating questions of professional responsibility like any questions of law in other law school courses. Students are taught from rules, statutes, cases, problems, and excerpts from books and articles from law reviews and other periodicals. Law teaching generally focuses on judicial or administrative decisions in cases or on problems taken from actual disputes or created for the purpose of discussion. Rules, statutes, and restatements of the law by the American Law Institute are also studied, but usually in the context of problems or cases. Discussion is supplemented by reference to law journal articles and the writings of philosophers and social scientists. The purpose of the course in the legal profession is not only to make the students familiar with the relevant regulatory material,[5] but also to get them to think about the unresolved and difficult problems in the field, to prepare them to face and deal with such problems when they move from the protection of law school to the real world of law practice.

The content of courses in legal ethics focuses on the rules governing lawyer conduct and explores their implications for the freedom of lawyers to serve clients. Some would go further and add concerns about "ethics in general" to the course material. The latter would emphasize both the areas in which the lawyer has discretion (and is therefore ethically responsible for decisions) and the ways in which the lawyer might face and deal with problems not dealt with by the applicable rules. In these discussions, teachers and students have had to face the often inchoate, fluid, and contestable nature of ethical principles, the great diversity in ethical and meta-ethical thinking, and the individualist bias in our social system which tends to relegate questions of ethics to the individual and condemn the imposition of one's own ethical principles on others.[6] They have also had to face the problems that arise when a lawyer's own ethical standards prohibit what the law allows her to do for the client, and the client has (arguably) a right to the lawyer's assistance in accomplishing, or when a lawyer's ethical standards insist on aiding the client in a way prohibited by the applicable regulations.[7] There is another difficulty with discussing the ethical conduct of lawyers, the degree to which the lawyer's ethics, even when they are freed from the particular constraints of professional rules, are role-differentiated rather than "general." That is, are the personal ethics of a lawyer the ethics of Everyman, or are they the ethics of a person in a particular role?

In some law schools, legal ethics are also discussed in other courses, such as contracts, torts, property, corporations, remedies, and civil procedure. Materials have been published to aid instructors in various courses that do not focus on legal ethics, to integrate discussion of legal ethics into course discussion.[8] The first problem in such courses is to determine just what "ethics" are to be talked about. Should the discussion be limited to the effect the applicable rules governing lawyer conduct have on the representation of clients with problems in that area of the law, or should it include ethics in a broader sense of that term? The second problem is how to fit such discussion into a course in which the focus is on the teaching of rules of law and their application in diverse cases. Keeping the discussion of ethics too separate would cause the students to encapsulate that material and store it as interesting but not important. Mixing the discussion of ethics too intimately into the discussion of the course material would tend to muddy up the students' understanding and ability to work with the applicable rules and practices in the field on which the course is supposed to focus.

At St. Louis University School of Law, problems of lawyers' ethics are raised in three ways. All entering students go through a two-day course in professional ethics.[9] There is also an exit program in legal ethics for those graduating students who elect to participate in it.[10] There is a required course in legal profession,[11] which is taught for either two or three semester hours by one of three faculty members. In addition, legal ethics, both in terms of the rules governing lawyers and the ethics of people in the practice of law, are discussed in other courses in law school, such as courses in property, business associations, remedies, and civil procedure.

Appendix

Introduction and two problems from the
materials for the
Thomas Deline Program on Ethics
for Entering Law Students

I. Introduction

A. Purpose

This program is an attempt to introduce you to the ethical context in which persons represent and assist others in seeking the latters' ends, and to impress on you the controversial nature of any statement about ethics or the ethical quality of a person or action.

Not all of the problems you will consider involve the practice of law. The purpose of this course is not to teach you the law of law practice or the applicable rules of conduct for lawyers. Rather, this course is designed to confront you with ethical problems of the sort that both lawyers and nonlawyers face. In the course of the discussion you may want to consider whether it should really make much difference that the person dealing with the problem is (or is not) functioning as a lawyer. To understand some of the problems, you will need to know something of the substantive legal context in which they arise. Don't let that bother you. The discussion leader and the materials relevant to the problem will provide what law you will need to work through the problem.

B. Organization

On the first day, there will be a lecture to introduce the material and provide a framework for discussions in the subsequent discussion sessions. After the lecture, and a short break, you will meet with the discussion group to which you have been assigned. You will learn of your assignment to a discussion group during the break after the lecture. In that group you will discuss the first and (after a short break) the second problems provided with these materials. Each session should take no more than one hour.

The second day of this course starts with another lecture, after which you will meet with a new discussion group (to which you have been assigned). As on the previous day, you will learn of your assignment to a group during the break after the lecture. There will be one session with this discussion group. You will be presented with the final problem in this set. Again, the lecture should provide some framework for approaching the problems. At the end of this session, you will meet for refreshments and informal discussion with other participants in this program.

C. A Paper

One week from the last class, a short (not more than five pages) paper will be due, which will provide (a) a well-organized and informative summary and discussion of the work of the discussion groups in which you participated during the two days of this program and (b) an evaluation of the program in terms of its goals and the success of the program in meeting them.

Why is a paper assigned? After all, five pages are probably in-adequate space in which to capture all of what was to be accomplished by the program. Moreover, the time given to write the paper is too short for the necessary reflection and development of ideas. One reason for the paper is to provide a way in which you can begin to organize your thoughts about what has transpired in the course of this program, and about your own response to it. The time you have to write this paper is about right for that. There is another good reason for the assignment of a paper. Your paper will be read and commented on by a person who has been trained as a lawyer. This will be your first, and most painless, chance to check your skills at organization and exposition of ideas.

II. Problems

The following problems can be discussed profitably without any knowledge of law. Problem 2 requires some small understanding of judicial procedure. For the purpose of discussing problem 2, all you need to know is this: A judgment is a final adjudication of all related issues between the parties (the plaintiff and the defendant). In other words, if the judgment is fairly arrived at, by proper procedure before an impartial judge, the defendant is no longer allowed to deny liability to the plaintiff, even if the defendant did not put on any evidence. So, in problem 2, once the default judgment becomes final against the defendant, the latter is stuck insofar as liability is concerned, unless the default judgment is set aside.

Problem 1: The Tennis Tournament

The Men's Intercity Tennis League consists of four tennis clubs in two cities. Each year, one of the clubs sponsors a tournament for the league. Each competition between clubs consists of three singles and four doubles matches, so eleven people are needed each week to compete. The matches are played on Sunday afternoon. Each match is between similarly ranked opponents. That is, the top singles player from one club plays the top singles player from the other in singles match #1, and the third-ranked doubles team from one club plays the third-ranked doubles team from the other club in doubles match #3. All singles matches and doubles match #1 are played at 12:30 P.M. and doubles matches #2 to #4 are played at 1:30 P.M. The following Saturday is reserved in case of rain. Because of tennis court scheduling difficulties, no other makeup time is available. Each club that wins its competition receives a trophy. The club whose teams win its competition by the greatest margin receives the "championship" trophy. The other winning club receives the "winner" trophy. To receive either trophy is considered a major event by these clubs.

This story is about a match between the Pinebrook Athletic Club and the City Athletic Association (C.A.A.). Gary is the unofficial captain of the Pinebrook squad. He was "chosen" by default because he was willing to make the arrangements for the match. Hank is the captain of the City Athletic Association's players. He was probably selected in the same way as Gary was. Between these two organizations there is a friendly but intense rivalry.

On Sunday, May 21, the tennis players from Pinebrook traveled to the City Athletic Association's courts to begin the tournament. After the first few matches, it began to rain. The opponents were ahead on points. After a while it began to pour, and the next matches were postponed to the next Saturday, May 27, with the same players resuming from the point at the match at which they had left off. At the end of the day, the C.A.A. led the competition 3 matches to 2. They had won all the singles matches and Pinebrook won the #1 and #2 doubles matches. All that remained to be played Saturday were #3 and #4 doubles matches. To win, Gary's team had to win both doubles matches, and Gary doubted that this would happen. The #3 doubles team was questionable. There was plenty of heart, but they were erratic. Sometimes they were great, sometimes not. On the basis of what he knew about the opposing #4 doubles team, Gary was confident that his #4 team would win.

During the week of May 22nd, Gary was told that one of the players on the Pinebrook #4 doubles team would be out of town and could not change his plans. If that match were to be forfeited, the whole tournament would be lost to the other club. Even if the #3 teams won, the forfeiture of the #4 doubles match would give the victory to C.A.A., 4 matches to 3. Still, Gary did not give up hope. After all, a lot of things can change in a week. On Friday the 26th, more bad news hit. A player in the #3 doubles team telephoned Gary to say that he had to attend a funeral on Saturday and could not be at the match. Now, Pinebrook would forfeit both matches. The situation was made known to the rest of the club's players. They all understood that, if the two players did not show up, the entire tournament would be lost.

As Gary prepared to call Hank and admit defeat, Gary's telephone rang. It was Hank. Hank told Gary that two of his players would be unable to play Saturday. One of the players was from the #3 doubles team and the other was from the #4 doubles team. With those games forfeited by Hank's team, Gary's team would take the cup.

To give his team a victory, all Gary had to do was accept the forfeitures in the two doubles games and tell Hank nothing about his own club's inability to produce a #3 and a #4 team. You are Gary. What do you tell Hank?

Questions for Problem 1

1.   What is Gary's position when he receives the telephone call?

    a.   Does it make a difference whether he is acting as an individual, a teammate, a team captain, or all of these things?

    b.   Consider a slightly different story. The game is between Gary and Hank for the championship of the city. There is only one day and one time available for the game. Gary discovers that he won't be able to play because of a flare-up of an old injury. He decides to call Hank and tell him. Before he can pick up the telephone, Hank calls up and tells Gary that he (Hank) can't make it. Does Gary tell Hank?

2.   Gary knows that if Hank's teams do not show up, his club wins by forfeiture. How does he know that?

    a.   Where do the rules of forfeiture come from? How do you know when a competition is forfeited?

    b.   Why have rules of forfeiture? What purpose do they serve?

    c.   Is it arguable that Hank's telephone call, itself, amounted to a forfeiture? If it did, then there is no reason for Gary to tell Hank anything, is there? Does this interpretation of the forfeiture rules make sense in terms of their function? Does it comport with the generally understood approach to forfeiture (or does that matter)?

3.   What rules guide your evaluation of Gary's behavior with respect to Hank in this situation? The rules of tennis? The rules about forfeiture? The rules that govern the conduct of sports competitors? The rules that govern ordinary behavior in society? Insofar as this situation is concerned, do these rules differ? Does reference to one set of rules exclude reference to any other set?

4.   Consider the situation under ordinarily applicable ethical standards, which condemn dishonesty. If Gary does not tell Hank about the situation with his team, is he being dishonest?

   a.   If Gary says nothing, how can he be dishonest?

   b.   Assume Gary has some discretion as to what to do. If he decides he may tell Hank, must he tell Hank before the next day?

5.   How should Gary decide what he should do? Gary hates to lose and takes great pride in his club.

   a.   Does it matter that the team members already assumed they would lose by default? Should that be enough to let Gary tell Hank?

   b.   Should Gary assume that the teammates would want him to refuse to tell Hank?

   c.   If Gary assumes that his teammates would want him to refuse to tell Hank, how should that affect Gary's decision what to do?

   d.   If Gary assumes that his teammates would accept it if Gary told Hank, how should that affect Gary's decision what to do?

   e.   Should Gary involve his teammates in the decision? How should he put the issue to be decided?

6.   What has this problem got to do with lawyering? Gary plays two roles here: captain and team member. As captain, he plays a representative role. Do special moral or ethical standards apply to Gary as captain different from those that apply to Gary as team player? If they do, do they include a duty to pursue victory for the team by means in addition to assuring a fair schedule and encouraging good play? Reconsider your answer to question 1. Compare Gary's position to that of John Strait in problem 2. In both cases, the question of victory comes up and is important. Is victory independently valuable in both cases? Is the value of victory for the represented party sufficiently strong to trump all other moral/ethical considerations?

Problem 2: Winning

On December 27, 1992, Harry Blesse was injured when a cart, which was rented from the Gross Building Materials Company, tipped over and threw drywall onto him. Blesse was hospitalized and lost a substantial amount of time at work. After he left the hospital, Blesse went to the office of John Strait, a lawyer in private practice, who specializes in personal injury, commercial fraud, and domestic relations litigation. Strait heard Blesse's story. He indicated that he had some doubts about the likelihood of success against the only solvent defendant—Gross Building Materials Company—but said he would accept the case on a 40% contingency fee basis.

After some investigation, Strait drew up a petition which set out a claim against Gross Building Materials Company. He filed the petition with the clerk of court on May 3, 1993. Personal service of the summons and petition was had on the defendant's president, Wilfred Gross, on Friday, May 7. On the following Monday, May 10, Gross's secretary walked the papers over to the offices of the company's liability insurer. The clerk who received the papers from Gross's secretary immediately copied the documents, put the copy in a file, and sent the original by runner to the law offices of Fee & Garbie, to be given to Hektor Fee, who normally represented Gross Building Materials Company and other similar businesses who were insured against liability by the insurance company.

Not knowing who defense counsel was, nor having received any papers that indicated that the defense intended to do anything about the lawsuit, Strait moved for a judgment of default on Friday, May 28. On Monday, May 31, Strait put on evidence to support the amount of damages claimed, and an order granting an interlocutory judgment of default (that is, a temporary judgment, pending the issuance of a permanent judgment) was entered on the same day. A notice of the motion and a verbatim report of that judgment were printed in the Daily Record for Wednesday, June 2. Unless the court withdrew its interlocutory judgment before then, the judgment would be final against the defendant at the close of business (4:30 P.M.) on June 22.

On June 10, Fee's answer on behalf of the defendant, Gross Building Materials Company, was filed with the circuit court, and a copy was sent to plaintiff's counsel, Strait. Strait called his client, Blesse, and told him that he had received a copy of the answer filed in his case, but that it was filed too late. If defendant's counsel does not move to set aside the interlocutory default by June 22, a final judgment of default would issue against the defendant. Before the 22nd, it would be fairly easy to set aside the interlocutory default judgment and allow the defendant to file an answer, so long as the defendant shows that the reason for lateness is not the gross or culpable fault of that party or counsel. However, if a final judgment of default is entered, the court is not likely to set it aside if the grounds for setting it aside do not indicate truly extraordinary and unavoidable circumstances.

Strait then asked his client what he should do. Should he inform counsel for the defendant that an interlocutory judgment for default was entered, or should he just sit on the case for 20 more days and then move for a final judgment of default? Blesse was puzzled. "What if you tell the other side and the court lets them go ahead? We can still win, can't we?" Strait answered: "We can, but as I told you when I took this case, it is awfully dicey. We could lose on the question of liability." "Oh," said Blesse, " I guess you should just keep quiet then, right?" "If that is your instruction," said Strait, after which he wished his client a good afternoon and hung up the telephone. Strait waited the necessary time, and a few days extra, before going to court and filing his motion to enter a final judgment by default in the amount of $1,5 million. The motion was granted the following Monday. Shortly thereafter, Strait informed Fee of the final judgment.

Fee filed a motion to set aside the default judgment and to allow him to file his answer late. Fee's motion was accompanied by several affidavits, setting out what occurred between the time his office received the petition in this case and the filing of the final default judgment. A copy of the motion and affidavits was sent to Strait. In summary, the motion and affidavits set out a credible story of how a very well-organized and effective system for following cases and checking on deadlines broke down in two places. First, the secretary of the lawyer to whom the defense was assigned mislaid the papers to be filed with the court and sent them to the insurance company with the original and a copy of the answer to be filed. Then, a claims manager at the insurance company, who received the pleadings for approval and signature, mislaid all the papers. His secretary found them and sent them directly to Fee, who told his law clerk to file them with copies to the lawyer for the plaintiff. No one pointed out to Fee that the papers were late, and that he should check to see if a default had been entered, and file a motion for permission to file late. That is why the answer was filed on June 10 without any accompanying motions.

At argument on the motion to set aside the default judgment, the judge noted that the motion filed by Fee would have been successful without doubt, had it been filed before the 22nd of June. However, as was forcefully argued by Strait, the grounds for setting aside the judgment entered on the default were much stricter and it was quite plain from the affidavits and the motion that they were insufficient. So, Fee lost his motion and Strait won a judgment for his client.

Questions for Problem 2

For the discussion of this problem, you are not expected to know anything about the duties of lawyers to their clients, except insofar as those duties are dealt with in the materials for this course.

1.   What is Strait's position in this lawsuit? How is it like Gary's in problem 1? How is it different from Gary's position?

2.   What if Strait had informed defense counsel that the latter was out of time and that Strait intended to seek a judgment on default if defense counsel did not file an answer before the time to ask for such a judgment arrived? Would that be a betrayal of his client? Would it be ethically wrong?

3.   What if defense counsel suddenly realized that time for filing an answer had passed and called Strait and asked for an extension of a week to file the answer? The usual way in which this is done is for defense and plaintiff's counsel to join in a motion for leave to extend the time for filing to a specified date.

a.   May Strait agree to the extension if it is requested by the other side? Another way of asking this question is whether Strait must fight for every procedural advantage. Of course, if Strait decides that it is in the long-term interest of his client not to pursue particular positions, even though winning them might provide some short-term advantage, then his decision not to pursue them is easily justified in terms of the single-minded pursuit of his client's ends, which include victory. What if he agrees to the extension out of courtesy, or a sense of fairness to the other side? Is that permitted?

b.   If you think Strait may agree to the extension because it is the right thing to do, how is this different from telling the opponent that time is about to run? If you think Strait may not agree to the extension if it is not plainly in his own client's interests to do so, then do you reject the relevance of any concept of consideration for others or fair play in this context?

4.   Try a slightly different story—one in which the defendant did file in time, but under the wrong case number. Strait knows about the misfiling. When the time for default comes up, Strait goes to court and asks for a judgment. Under the rules of court, there is no requirement that the party moving for judgment on default notify the opposing counsel of the motion or the date of hearing on the motion. Should Strait have notified opposing counsel anyway? If you answer that he should,

how is this case different from the case to which this question is appended? See *Owens v. Neely*, 866 S.W.2d 716 (Tex. App. Houston, 1993)

5.   Let's return to the problem of Strait's role as an advocate. Just what should Strait do when representing a client? What is he allowed to do?

a.   Is he hired to win for the client, no matter what? Is he hired to obtain the best possible result by way of settlement or trial? Are these two ideas of what he is supposed to do different from one another in any significant way?

b.   If he is hired to win for the client, no matter what, does that mean that he must do anything he can to win for the client? There are limits to what the lawyer may do as an advocate. He may not act contrary to law, and he may not counsel or assist his client in fraudulent or illegal conduct. Why these limitations? If these, why not others?

c.   Are there ethical constraints on what a person may do to aid another? There are such constraints set out in statutes and court-adopted rules governing lawyers' conduct. The lawyer may not bribe or intimidate the judge or jurors; help anyone lie to the court; or engage in fraudulent or deceitful conduct. Are there also background rules of fair play—rules that apply to everyday life, to which you might refer in default of more specifically assigned rules? Would such background rules aid in interpreting statutes and rules of professional conduct?

d.   Should Strait be limited by what his client could do? Would Blesse be equally justified in doing what you felt Strait is allowed (required?) to do in Blesse's behalf?

6.   Is a lawyer ever justified in trying to "push" the client to pursue a particular course of action? Does it matter whether the "push" is in the direction that leads to victory, or whether it is in the direction of "the right thing to do" in this case? Consider this case:

7.   Your client has succeeded in obtaining a default judgment against the defendant. The defendant has appealed on very weak grounds. Your client telephones you and says, "I don't want to go any further. Let's just drop the whole thing!" What should you do? Do you try to find out why your client wants to drop the lawsuit? Why should you inquire into your client's motives?

8.   Assume that a person came to your office and asked for your help in a matter. You discover that the person is asking for help which would harm the interests of a client of yours.

a.   Do you sit and listen to the person, asking leading questions to obtain information that would help your client, or do you tell the person that you cannot help him and advise him to say no more?

b. If the period of limitations is running on that person's claim, may you tell him so? If you may, should you?

9.   Part of the difficulty in problems 1 and 2 has to do with honesty and lying. What counts as dishonest in one context might not count as dishonest in another. Was Strait honest with his opponent? Was Gary honest with his? Consider this variation on problem 2: Shortly after the time for filing the answer has passed, Fee calls Strait and tells him that he (Fee) is going to file an amended answer. If the original answer were filed on time, the amended answer would raise no problems of timing. Strait answers: I have no objection to that. Does whether or not that was an honest answer depend on whether, in the context of the exchange (that is, between lawyers in the positions of Fee and Strait), Strait's response implied that the initial answer was timely filed. Was Strait lying to Fee in this context?

Notes

[1] From the early days of legal education there has been a course in "legal ethics." It covered rules governing lawyers in the practice of law. Violation of these rules could result in the temporary or permanent removal of a person's license to practice law. Initially, they were called "canons of legal ethics," a body of hortatory statements of principle from which were derived grounds for the disciplining of lawyers—especially those who advertised and solicited legal work. Later, these canons were replaced by a more detailed "code of professional responsibility" which distinguished between "disciplinary rules" and "ethical considerations," the former being grounds for lawyer discipline. The successor to this "code" is called "rules of professional conduct" which does not purport to have anything to do with ethics.

[2] The course in legal ethics or professional responsibility was not generally required of law students until the 1970s. Then, law schools started out by limiting this required course to one credit hour in a single semester. Now, the usual course in legal ethics is a one-semester course of two or three credit hours, and includes other aspects of the law governing lawyers.

[3] This duty is not usually referred to as an "ethical," but rather as a "professional" duty.

[4] A "pervasive" approach to legal ethics is being promoted. There is now a book of cases, problems, and materials on legal ethics adapted to use in particular courses in law school, as a supplement to the "normal" materials for that course. See Deborah L. Rhode, *Professional Responsibility, Ethics by the Pervasive Method*, 2nd ed. (New York: Aspen Law and Business, 1998). A more specific treatment of what is done at St. Louis University School of Law will be provided *infra*.

[5] The relevant regulatory material is actually the regulatory material for each state and federal court. The material discussed in law school is normally taken from the model sets of regulations published by the American Bar Association, a version of which is adopted in almost all the states and the federal courts. They are the Model Rules of Professional Conduct and its predecessor, the Model Code of Professional Responsibility. The opinions issued by a committee of the ABA interpreting the Model Rules of Professional Conduct are authoritative in those states that have adopted these rules.

[6] And even here, we fail because the truly relevant regulatory material is state law, and varies from state to state in sometimes quite important ways. The law school course tends to focus on the common features of American law and only occasionally considers the law of a particular state. Law graduates are expected to practice, not only in Missouri or Illinois, but in any jurisdiction in the United States (any state or the District of Columbia) and occasionally more than one jurisdiction. Some of our graduates also concern themselves with the laws of international organizations and foreign countries. Some faculty and students have perceived the paradox of the positivistic/individualistic position with respect to the subjectivity of ethics, which at the same time imposed its own ethics—the duty of loyalty and the prohibition on imposing one's ethical beliefs on others—on lawyers.

[7] For example, a lawyer is prohibited from counseling or assisting a client in the violation of law. This prohibition stands against the lawyer's advising or participating in civil disobedience. The problem of civil disobedience leads fairly quickly to the question, whether there is a moral obligation to obey law, and the ethics of taking advantage of leeways in the applicable law for the sake of the client's achieving his ends and preserving the client's autonomy in the face of community (e.g., legal) limits on that autonomy.

[8] See n. 4, *supra*.

[9] See Appendix for materials for this program. The program includes lectures and small group discussions of problems that pose ethical dilemmas, with discussions led by practicing lawyers or instructors with substantial experience in the practice of law. It is financed by a gift from a law alumnus, Thomas Deline.

[10] This program, which I can make available to the reader, is similar to that for entering students and is also financed by a gift from Thomas Deline. It includes an address by a notable figure in the field of legal ethics who also participates in a program-ending discussion with students and discussion leaders. The first guest speaker was Geoffrey C. Hazard, Jr., professor of law at the University of Pennsylvania, and reporter for the ABA Model Rules of Professional Responsibility. He is also director of the American Law Institute. The second guest speaker was Charles W. Wolfram, professor of law at Cornell University, reporter for the American Law Institute's Restatement of the Law Governing Lawyers.

[11] Three instructors teach the course entitled Legal Profession. The coverage and emphasis in the course taught by one of them differs from that in the courses taught by the other two. All three courses focus primarily on the regulatory material, but bring up ethical concerns and, at least in one course, the possibility of defiance of the rules in some cases.

ETHICS AND PUBLIC SERVICE

James F. Gilsinan
College of Public Service

The mission of the College of Public Service is to help create public life, that is, the bringing together of people in order to achieve a common purpose. This focus provides the organizing theme that connects our various departments. The college consists of six departments: Communication Sciences and Disorders; Counseling and Family Therapy; Educational Studies; Leadership and Higher Education; Public Policy; and Research Methods. All of these disciplines make it possible for people to participate more effectively in a common enterprise, whether through improving their communication skills, knowledge, or physical and community surroundings.

The work of Harry C. Boyte and Nancy N. Kari suggests that bringing people together has four dimensions:[1]

SPACE—literally a commons where people from different places have equal access to a particular physical location. The great parks of London were specifically designed to provide such a space for city dwellers regardless of class standing or other resources.

DIVERSITY—as the example illustrates, public life assumes diversity, not similarity.

MUTUAL PROBLEM SOLVING—that creates visible, public change for the improvement of a particular condition. Unlike private life, public life is oriented toward change rather than security.

CATALYTIC LEADERSHIP—positional leadership, based on expertise or a formally held post, is replaced by catalytic leadership, leadership that calls people to become active in creating the commons, that which we all share. The catalytic role is one of P-r-o-p-h-e-t, rather than P-r-o-f-i-t. The private values of loyalty and consensus are replaced by peer accountability, that is, accountability that invites critique, debate, and reflection.

Each of these dimensions has an ethical component which, in its various majors and degrees, the College of Public Service consciously addresses.

Discussions of urban sprawl and growth management are not generally framed by an ethical dimension. More often such arguments are put in economic or legal terms; e.g., the right of individuals to live where they choose or the impact of outward growth on the economic vitality of the central city. The notion of "commons," however, clearly raises an ethical question for the college's students and faculty in urban planning, public administration, and urban affairs.

Should federal and state highway funds be used to ease the access of individuals to far-flung suburbs, increasing both auto traffic at the expense of public transportation and contributing to the emptying out of core cities? The $500 million Page Avenue extension that will ease traffic congestion between St. Louis County and St. Charles County in Missouri has caused considerable debate around these issues. The ethical components of the debate, however, remain largely unarticulated. Instead, the debates about this project have emphasized traffic flow, the development of St. Charles, the need to relieve congestion on the I–70 bridge, and so on. Ethically, the question can be posed, "Does the project contribute to the creation of a commons, a place where people of different races, classes, locations can come together to create a public life?"

The answer is not immediately evident. For example, there is no reason why a commons cannot be located in St. Charles. In fact, better transportation to and from the area may improve the chance for diverse people to gather. But in analyzing some of the arguments against the extension, one hears echoes of privatization, or the closing off of the chance for a public life, a commons. Thus, such an extension will bring "those" people out here. Whoever those people are remained fairly undefined, but what is clear was they are not like the folks there. Indeed, this was a major argument against extending Metrolink, a light fixed rail system, to the region.

The failure to create a public life with a commons for diverse people to gather and work on unifying tasks is evident in Kosovo. Failure to raise ethical questions around the notion of what contributes to and detracts from the commons has serious consequences, a point we attempt to underscore for our students.

The commons assumes diversity, but not just racial or economic diversity. For a commons to exist, it must attract and support people with diverse ideas as well. A recent case study by Dr. Claire McCown from our Department of Leadership and Higher Education illustrates the point.[2] A particular school district was sponsoring a career week where parents of the children were encouraged to address classes on their careers and career preparation. A young girl whose mother was a black-jack dealer on one of the casino boats was told, after she volunteered her mom for a session, that her mother could not address the class about her job. The principal felt that gambling was too controversial a profession to talk about in the schools. Now your private ethics may be opposed to gambling, but the fact that the school district received considerable tax revenue from the boats, and that many people in the district were employed by the industry, makes this case one of public life and ethics as well. This job incidently caused the mother to get off welfare and become economically independent. So the public life aspect of the principal's decision is fairly clear. In this context, should the mother have been allowed to talk about her job? What if the mom had been a bartender or worked for the tobacco industry? Public life requires the exposure and debate of different ideas, not censorship. The latter fails to promote public life and work. Unfortunately, there is an increasing number of examples of diversity in public life being thwarted, often in the name of religious doctrinal purity.

The withdrawal of an invitation to a prominent state politician to address the graduating class at a local Catholic high school, and a similar withdrawal of an invitation to a former mayor of the City of Saint Louis to receive an award from a Catholic athletic association, illustrate the point. The invitations were withdrawn, not because of a specific topic they would address at the respective ceremonies, but because of opinions they had expressed regarding reproductive rights in other forums. Ethically, these withdrawals are questionable because they fail to support diversity of thought necessary for public life.

The notion of mutual problem solving is captured by the Jesuit ideal of companions. As you all know, St. Ignatius called his original followers "companions." It is an interesting word. It comes from two Latin words, "com" meaning together, and "panis" meaning bread. Literally, it means "one who eats bread with another." Our students and faculty work in very diverse communities. The temptation is to approach those communities as experts, whether in education, counseling, urban development, or as clinicians. I quote directly from an ethics case study by Drs. Mary Domahidy and Karen Caldwell of Public Policy Studies and Counseling and Family Therapy respectively, and Mike Penick, a graduate student in Public Policy, to illustrate the ethical issues surrounding the notion of professionalism in a community setting.[3] The story is based on an Afrocentric curriculum used at one of the schools where we work.

> When facing a closed door or opening, one stands outside and says, "Hodi, Hodi" to request to be admitted. Once inside, one is expected to speak to each person, starting with the eldest and then continuing by age.[4]

The authors go on to comment:

> To identify each person by name and by age requires in-depth knowledge of the community and its relationships. The outsider has to be present for some time in order to be able to accomplish such a task. This stands in dramatic contrast to the expectation that the professional can enter a community, define an appropriate role, and offer expert knowledge. The idea, though, that the outsider will significantly impact the lives of those present underscores the need to reflect and recall the tenet to "do no harm" as the core professional stance.[5]

Creating public life requires mutuality whereby the expert learns from, as well as contributes to, a common work. Otherwise experts risk doing harm or further disempowering those with whom we work.

Finally, the creation of public life requires catalytic leadership. Boyte and Kari contrast catalytic leadership with positional leadership, the kind most often associated with expertise, whereby the leader makes decisions, articulates vision, and mobilizes resources. We have already seen that this is ethically problematic for community work. They also compare catalytic leadership with communal leadership. Communal leadership emphasizes the facilitator role. Unfortunately, a facilitator in many community settings is more verbally skilled than the participants and therefore can subtly, if unintentionally, control the agenda. In this scenario, people are still disenfranchised, even if it is done nicely. According to Boyte and Kari, catalytic leadership "calls people to work of significance, taps new energy and spirit, frames large tasks, provides tools for work, and joins with others in public work."[6] Habitat for Humanity and community gardens represent real work that is led in a catalytic rather than a positional or communal way, and that helps build public life.

The College of Public Service supports research on case studies and these studies in turn are used in class settings to help students and faculty reflect on their practice in the community. There is a special burden on our students because they are trained in professions—teachers, clinicians, government specialists—that can, if handled incorrectly, inhibit rather than contribute to public life. If they become experts who are not reflective practitioners, conscious of the ethical dimensions of their work, they are in positions to do great harm to individuals, families, and communities. Thus, practice must be accompanied by reflection. It is this triangulation of classroom knowledge, community practice, and reflection that inform the educational practice of the College of Public Service.

Notes

[1] See Harry C. Boyte and Nancy N. Kari, *Building America: The Democratic Promise of Public Work* (Philadelphia: Temple University Press, 1996); and "Leadership and Public Work—An Alternative to Service Learning" (A Workshop for Leadership Education . . . Across the Campus and Beyond, Arlington, Virginia, April 9–11, 1999).

[2] Claire McCown, "An Ethical Case Study with Exercises for Cross Discipline Use," in *Using Case Studies in the Classroom* (Ethics Committee for the College of Public Service, Saint Louis University, December 4, 1998, mimeographed).

[3] Mary Domahidy, Karen Caldwell, and Mike Penick, "Preparing Professionals in Community Settings," in *Using Case Studies in the Classroom* (Ethics Committee for the College of Public Service, Saint Louis University, December 4, 1998, mimeographed).

[4] Ibid., 23.

[5] Ibid.

[6] Harry C. Boyte and Nancy N. Kari, "Leadership and Public Work—An Alternative to Service Learning."

WHAT'S ETHICS GOT TO DO WITH PUBLIC HEALTH?

Fostering Professional Ethics and Social Responsibility in Public Health

Sharon M. Homan
School of Public Health

Introduction

I'll begin with our question—"What's Ethics Got to Do with It?" The "It" is the profession of Public Health, and the academic dimensions of education, research, and practice. To address this question, I will use the praxis circle (experience—*see*, reflection—*judge*, action—*act*) as a hermeneutic tool to interpret the question and respond to the challenge of examining and imagining the role of ethics in graduate education in public health. I will consider two interrelated aspects of this challenge. One aspect is what I will call professional ethics. The second aspect is the ethics of a profession, or what I will call social responsibility.

Examining Professional Ethics in Public Health

The World Health Organization defines health as "a state of complete physical, mental and social well-being and not merely the absence of disease or infirmity."[1] The health of the public goes beyond the medical traditions of individual diagnosis, treatment, and cure to societal approaches to the promotion of health and the prevention of disease and injury among diverse populations and communities. The field of bioethics is linked to the medical traditions, with a traditional focus on ethical aspects of clinical practice in medicine, nursing, and psychology. Within the field of health, there has been a growing body of literature exploring ethical approaches and methods suited for public health. Over the last few decades, there has been a renewed interest in ethics within the public health professional community, including the

Association of Schools of Public Health, the American College of Epidemiology, the Centers for Disease Control, and the National Institutes of Health. Epidemiologists have taken the lead in these efforts.[2] The "developments in professional ethics in epidemiology occurred against a background of social and political movements in the early 1990s that included vigorous efforts to assure that women and minorities are adequately represented in research projects funded by the National Institutes of Health."[3]

Before describing "what's ethics got to do with public health," I will describe the praxis of public health from the perspectives of the profession, the professional, and the academy.

The Public Health Profession

How does the public health profession "see, judge, and act" to ensure the public's health? The praxis model of "see, judge, act" is consistent with three core functions of public health: assessment, policy development, and assurance. Assessment (data collection, analysis, dissemination, and management) is seeing what are the current health problems that are real or potential threats to citizens. Policy development (planning, policy analysis and formulation, establishing legal authority, policy implementation and evaluation) is judging what are the community's public health priorities and making wise and prudent policies around disease prevention and health promotion. The central action of public health is to assure that these policies are carried out and that communities are healthy and safe places for individuals and families to grow and prosper. Assurance involves disease prevention, health protection and promotion, quality standards, and access to care.

The Public Health Professional

In our next iteration of the praxis circle, we enter as public health professionals. The professional enters and engages the community in various ways—as expert, consultant, resource person, educator, facilitator, evaluator, community organizer, clinical practitioner—with the desire to raise consciousness, assess needs, build coalitions, educate, provide or link services, or other activities. How does a public health professional "see, judge, and act"? How the professional sees the community and judges what and how to interact with the community to promote health depends on the local circumstances, the social and political context, the community's desires and needs, and the expertise and perspectives of the public health professional(s). Public health actions, often called initiatives, take place within all realms of society and involve individual, institutional, neighborhood, community, congregational, city, county, state, national, and global approaches. Initiatives are wide-ranging and multidisciplinary, emphasizing such issues as: improvement and redesign of health services integration and delivery; control of diseases such as cancer, heart disease, and stroke; prevention and immunization programs in schools and work sites; cessation of risky behaviors such as smoking, excess alcohol, adolescent sexual activity, and substance abuse; maternal and child health; outreach and intervention in populations at risk such as the aged, homeless persons, persons with disabilities, and the mentally ill; reduction in family and community violence; clean air and water; adequate and safe housing; immunization and screening; health communication; and HIV prevention and policymaking.

How do public health professionals understand the experience of the public's health? What we have in common as public health professionals is that our focus is on the public, that is, on populations and communities. Our view is ecological—what does it take to promote human health and flourishing in community? It takes clean air and water, safe schools, absence of tobacco billboards, gun control, good housing, walking trails, religious and social networks, and the list goes on. Public health professionals look at the distribution of health risks, diseases, and resources across various subpopulations. We try to explain the relationships between risk factors and disease, and establish the effectiveness of health promotion and intervention strategies. Strategies include community development, regulation, improved access to health care, health care management, behavioral interventions, environmental efforts, school and workplace safety, health communication, policy development, etc. It is not surprising that public health professionals are a diverse group—epidemiologists, behavioral geneticists, biostatisticians, physicians, health educators, lawyers, ethicists, sociologists, behavioral scientists, health services researchers, toxicologists, environmental scientists, industrial hygienists, community psychologists, parasitologists, experts in economics, finance, health care organization, and health policy. Each has a different lens for seeing and understanding the health of the public.

"What's Ethics Got to Do with It?" That is, what does ethics have to do with the profession and the professional in relationship to the health of the public? From the perspective of individual members in a community or population, personal autonomy and the associated individual rights are the principal ethical norms and values for guiding decision making regarding the amelioration of risk. On the other hand, the community perspective on the origins of health needs focuses on the differential risks that exist for different groups as a function of the availability of opportunities and resources for maximizing their health. Norms of reciprocity, trust, and social obligation acknowledge the webs of interdependence and mutual support and caring that are essential for minimizing the risks of poor physical, psychological, or social health. Poor health results because communities fail to invest in and assume responsibility for the collective well-being of their members.[4]

Public Health in the Academy

We have moved through the praxis circle twice, first to examine the role of the profession of public health, and second, to examine the role of the public health professional. Next, we turn to the academy and look at the role of faculty. Our insertion into public health is as educators and researchers in a School of Public Health (SPH), and in the only school of public health in the U.S. sponsored by a Catholic university. We are a faculty of about 30 men and women, with diversity in academic training, degrees, and disciplines, race, culture, faith traditions, family structures, research interests, and faculty responsibilities. Thus, we each see the public's health with different lenses, have different theological and philosophical bases for our work, and have different lived experiences in the community. Each of us uses different theories, methods, and tools for teaching, research, and community practice.

What does ethics have to do with the work that we do? Many aspects of our work, individually and collectively, require moral reasoning and ethical decision making. Faculty analyze, reflect, and debate ethical considerations in their research and in the classroom. Ethical theories, principles, and case-based methods are used. Ethical issues include: informed consent in public health research (e.g., intentional nondisclosure of cocaine use among homeless shelter clients); randomized controlled trials in community settings; conflicting interests and research sponsorship; and the proper use of data to inform policy or provide expert witness. For example, the research of Drs. Ross Brownson and Doug Luke in the School of Public Health Prevention Research Center examines the health impacts of tobacco, the effect of tobacco advertising, and the need to control tobacco sales. Their research is relevant to tobacco policy and its impact on government, the tobacco industry, and retailers. A related and pressing ethical concern for Missourians is that the state may lose $9.6 million in federal block grants for drug and alcohol treatment because Missouri has not met its targets for reducing sales to minors. Is it ethical to sanction the state and reduce access to substance abuse treatment? Other issues are paternalism and individual rights versus the public good in public measures such as water fluoridation, disease surveillance, lead and mosquito abatement, immunization, seat belt enforcement, and international vaccine trials.

Another hot ethical area is genetic research and testing. For example, Dr. William True raised the following questions in a discussion about his recent work that establishes a genetic link to alcohol and tobacco addictive behavior.[5] Can this work lead to medicalization of a social problem, lead to insurance or work discrimination? Or, as genetic markers are developed, what will be the impact on families and their decisions about child bearing? Other faculty are involved in ethical reasoning related to establishing HIV prevention programs and policies for care and treatment; allocation of scarce resources and health care reform; value conflicts in social policies for promoting health (needle exchange, abortion, industrial air pollution control); and guidelines for mammography screening.

In terms of graduate education, all students are required to take an ethics course from the Center for Health Care Ethics. Equally important, all faculty bring ethical discussions and case studies to bear on subject matter being taught in each of our courses.

Understanding Our Social Responsibilities

Having examined "What's ethics got to do with it?" from the vantage of professional ethics in public health, I now move to a second aspect of the question: ethics of a profession and social responsibility. Here, I want to outline the importance of three aspects of the ethics of a profession: character formation, institutional culture, and inter-disciplinary discourse around issues of social justice.

Character Formation and Reflective Practice

William J. Byron explains the etymology of the term "character" as follows: "The Greek word *ethos*, the root form of *ethica* (ethics), referred to a person's fundamental orientation toward life. Originally, the word meant a dwelling place. With Aristotle, it came to mean an inner dwelling place or what we have come to call character."[6] An ethical public health professional is a person of sound character, marked by virtues and sensitive to justice issues. Professional codes of ethics are essential, but they are not sufficient.

The reflective public health professional wants to ask: "What do I stand for?" "What is the meaning and value of my work?" "What does it mean to be human and to flourish in community?" "To whom and to what am I ultimately responsible?"

Institutional Culture

Douglas Weed, a senior epidemiologist and physician at the National Cancer Institute, and other scholars in public health have led the discourse on ethics and epidemiology and the public health sciences. Weed has criticized epidemiology as becoming a technology-bound depersonalized biomedical science. He advocates for integrating the humanities, and in particular ethical discourse, into the intellectual activity of public health with implications for curricular reform.[7] Other public health scientists in the academy challenge us to look beyond the curriculum, noting that we can't have reform without change. That is, we need a change in the teaching and learning environment, in professional socialization. "Traditionally, the main goal of education, especially at advanced and professional levels, is the development of the internal capacities of the individual, in other words, his or her cognitive and technical competence."[8] Socialization is learning the organized behavior required of a professional. Socialization is a developmental process of personal change and growth that happens largely indirectly within the socializing institution. The School of Public Health, as a socializing institution with a culture and environment, has far greater potential to socialize than does any individual faculty member. Therefore, we need to look at the norms and values operative in our schools' research and service programs.

Here is where I think our School of Public Health is unique. With imagination, institutional support, and discourse, the School of Public Health can more fully realize its potential to be a leader in public health professional education. Our mission and philosophy are similar to those of other schools of public health, but our philosophy has a unique dimension. Our philosophy states that "we create an ethical climate consistent with the University's Catholic and Jesuit heritage, a climate embodied in a Covenant that guides faculty, students, and staff in their daily activities."[9] This defines our socializing culture, our climate. Our covenant reads: "In light of our person-centered service mission, we seek to provide for those who constitute the School of Public Health an environment which cultivates love, responsibility, trust, acceptance, concern, personal development, balance, and partnership."[10] Ethics and professional formation are woven into our curriculum and lived out in our culture. The School of Public Health derives strength from its diversity, intellectual capacity, and shared commitment to public health leadership and scholarship, guided by the Jesuit mission and our covenant values.

The word "covenant" defines our obligation to one another and to the academy as more than contractual obligation. There is a social dimension, a dimension committing us to be in relationship and be critically reflective about the common good, and our common purpose. As an academic body of faculty, what do we stand for? What is the meaning and value of our collective work? What is our responsibility to maintain and strengthen the specific character of Saint Louis University, an institution as both Jesuit and as a university? The noun "university" "guarantees a commitment to that fundamental autonomy, integrity, and honesty" in our search for truth, and in our dedication to research, teaching, and the various forms of service that correspond to our cultural mission.[11] The adjective "Jesuit" requires that we both seek knowledge for its own sake but, regularly ask, "knowledge for what?"[12] Our public health ecological perspective is that our knowledge leads to protecting and promoting human health and human flourishing in communities.

Interdisciplinary Discourse

Between 1990 and 1994, I was the co-PI of a $3.5 million NIAAA-funded research demonstration project. Fourteen projects were funded by support provided under the McKinney Homeless Assistance Act of 1987. Our project, called *Families with a Future*, involved designing, implementing, and evaluating interventions to assist homeless mothers, who had chemical dependencies, to secure economic and residential stability and reduce or stop their use of alcohol, cocaine, and other drugs, and improve the development of their children. As we designed and implemented the service and research components of our projects, we deliberated over several issues that had important ethical dimensions—issues such as informed consent, paternalism, non-reporting of known drug use, access to services, randomization, and agency salary structures. The project was enormously complex and intellectually challenging.

In spite of effective recruitment and retention of clients, comprehensive case management services, and sound measurement of hundreds of intermediate and longer-term outcomes, we found no evidence that the innovative and comprehensive services were effective. How do you interpret these negative findings? Blame the women (they were likely treatment resistant)? Blame the lack of adequate housing? Blame St. Louis City and County for insufficient and ill-coordinated services? Blame the NIAAA for thinking we could demonstrate in 18 months that the lives of pimped and abused women, trapped in multigenerational poverty, with kids, cocaine addictions, little education, mental health problems, and dysfunctional families, can be turned around with a year of enhanced case management? Blame society for their "not in my backyard" policies and actions to keep these women out of their neighborhoods and their kids out of their schools? It was clear that "blaming" was a harmful and useless strategy. This experience led to ethical questions related to understandings of justice and social responsibility. Our question, "What does ethics have to do with it?" seemed daunting compared to the ethical questions that arose in the design and conduct of our study. We needed to look further at our understandings of social responsibility and our role as committed professionals, citizens, and communities of faith. Psychiatric epidemiology, behavioral theory, addiction research, and other disciplines, as well as the familiar methodological tools of public health, couldn't provide the necessary insights into the deeper social and economic roots of homelessness. Without these insights, public health intervention research on homelessness and addiction was not likely to bear fruitful results.

What was essential was a thorough social analysis. This experience led me to search for two years for a more complete understanding of homelessness. I spent time with clients, learned their stories and ways of knowing, learned from the writings of black womanist ethicists concerned about the plight of women who are poor and black, gathered insights from providers, learned the constraints of the systems and institutions serving the homeless, studied the politics of race, culture and ethnicity, the meaning of the black extended family, drug trafficking and prostitution, violence, organizational behavior of the social service agencies. I learned that to be a good professional, a skilled practitioner and educator in my field of biostatistics, and work in community settings, I needed to become a reflective practitioner. I had to learn the language and skills of public discourse, and bring my personal and institutional identity to bear on that discourse of how we can meet the moral demands of justice and mercy to care for the most vulnerable populations such as homeless children.

I am discovering that many of my colleagues, within and outside the School of Public Health, are studying and searching for ways to meet the health, social, legal, and housing needs of vulnerable populations of the elderly, impoverished communities, the HIV infected, those with mental illness and disabilities, abusing families, homeless persons, high-risk mothers and infants. Many of our colleagues here at Saint Louis University have made this "option for the poor" out of a desire to eliminate injustices in our society. They may not use the language of "option for the poor," but they consciously recognize that the "justice of a community is measured by its treatment of the powerless in society."[13]

The homeless project gave us the impetus to develop an interdisciplinary course in reflective practice for graduate and professional students. *Social Responsibility and the Professional* became a course where we could critically reflect on how our professions can contribute to the transformation of society toward greater levels of justice and how we, as professionals, can contribute to the renewal of American public life. It is clear that professional training in our disciplines is not enough to address society's major problems. We need to stretch our imaginations. The course, *Social Responsibility and the Professional*, was developed to begin this process. Faculty and students from the professions of law, social work, business, public policy, public health, theology, philosophy, and ethics participate in this ongoing dialogue.

Many academic administrators and faculty around the country are mourning the isolation of higher education from public life, and our lost sense of obligation to deal with society's needs and to be communities of discourse. Several participants in the 1998 Kettering Foundation *Seminar on Professions and Public Life* "spoke of a widespread shift in higher education from civic education, in its broadest sense, toward professional training."[14] Participants described higher education as a vehicle for individual economic advancement, and much less a vehicle for promoting the common good. Professional education at Saint Louis University is already a vehicle for promoting the common good, while providing excellent technical and professional training.

Notes

[1] World Health Organization, "Constitution of the World Health Organization," *Basic Documents* 42nd ed. (Geneva: World Health Organization, 1999), 1.
[2] Steven S. Coughlin and Tom L. Beauchamp, *Ethics and Epidemiology* (New York: Oxford University Press, 1996), 18.
[3] Ibid.

[4] Lu Ann Aday, *At Risk in America: The Health and Health Care Needs of Vulnerable Populations in the United States* (San Francisco: Jossey-Bass Publishers, 1993), 2.

[5] William R. True, "Common Genetic Vulnerability for Nicotine and Alcohol Dependence in Men," *Archives of General Psychiatry* 56 (1999): 655–661.

[6] W. Byron, "Business: A Vocation to Justice and Love," in Francis A. Eigo, ed. *The Professions in Ethical Context: Vocations to Justice and Love* (Pennsylvania: Villanova University Press, 1986), 130. A more detailed discussion of the etymology of the term "character" may be found in James F. Drane, *Religion and Ethics* (New York: Paulist Press, 1976): 5–11.

[7] Douglas L. Weed, "Epidemiology, the Humanities and Public Health," *American Journal of Public Health* 85 (1995): 914–918.

[8] S. W. Bloom, "Editorial: Reform Without Change? Look Beyond the Curriculum," *AJPH* 85 (1995): 907–908.

[9] See Saint Louis University, School of Public Health, *Bulletin*, 1999.

[10] Ibid.

[11] Jesuits, *Documents of the Thirty-fourth General Congregation of the Society of Jesus: The Decrees of the General Congregation Thirty-Four, the Fifteenth of the Restored Society and the Accompanying Papal and Jesuit Documents* (St. Louis: Institute of Jesuit Sources, 1995), 191.

[12] Ibid.

[13] National Conference of Catholic Bishops, *Economic Justice for All: Pastoral Letter on Catholic Social Teaching and the U.S. Economy* (Washington, D.C.: National Conference of Catholic Bishops, 1987).

[14] Scott London, *Seminar on Professions and the Public Life* (Ohio: Charles F. Kettering Foundation, June 1998), 1–17.

TEACHING THE ETHICS OF TEACHING

James H. Korn
Center for Teaching Excellence

There are two aspects to including ethics across the curriculum. One concerns the content and methods of our teaching—the ethical issues that are present in our courses and how we help students to understand those issues. The second aspect concerns us as teachers—what we do and think about ethics. This article considers the second aspect, the ethics of teaching. It is important because we cannot expect students to take this topic seriously unless we do so first. We show the importance of ethics not just by raising questions and awareness in our classes, but also by being teachers who are aware of the ethical dilemmas that often face us and who have thought about what actions are right in various situations.

Most faculty never had a course on teaching, and many, including me, never had a course on ethics, so we had a lot to learn on our own in both areas. Today the situation appears to be changing with more research universities realizing the importance of preparing graduate students to teach and offering programs on teaching for faculty. One way this is being done at Saint Louis University is through the Center for Teaching Excellence (CTE), which began in 1992 as a resource center in a room in the corner of the Graduate School office suite. The staff worked primarily with graduate student assistants by providing them with emotional, as well as material, support. The number and range of our services have increased in recent years. These now include:

- Orientation programs for graduate assistants and for new faculty;
- A teaching certificate program that includes a series of seminars offered by experts;
- Faculty development in the use of technology in teaching; and
- A two-day workshop for untenured faculty to develop teaching portfolios.

Our mission is to serve as the heart of the Saint Louis University community of teachers and to express the spirit of that community by promoting the development of educational values in the Jesuit tradition. Certainly the teaching of ethics is part of that tradition, and the ethics of teaching should be among our concerns in the teaching center. In most, if not all, of our activities there are opportunities to consider ethical issues in teaching.

The Ethics of Teaching

The area of teaching that receives the most discussion in terms of ethical problems is our relationships with our students. The most extreme and dramatic cases are those in which a faculty member is accused of harassment of students. Sexual or emotional harassment clearly is wrong. However, the cases one reads about often involve misunderstandings and differing perspectives on what constitutes harassment, and then the ethical situation becomes muddier. A survey of psychology teachers' ethical practices used the phrase "boundary blurrings" in describing these situations.[1]

For example, what degree of social interaction with students is ethically acceptable? I should not ask a student to go with me to a romantic bed-and-breakfast, but may I ask that student to join me in Busch Center for coffee? What messages are contained in that invitation? For example, the student may perceive a relationship between her grade and the invitation, or see an opportunity to gain an advantage over other students. May I ask for a student's help in moving some books from my car to my office, or to help me wash my car, or baby-sit for my grandchildren? At what point does an expectation of common courtesy become exploitation?

Our preferences for some students over others raise another set of ethical issues. There is a vast social psychological literature on interpersonal attraction—why we like some people more than others. For example, we like people who are attractive and who are similar to us in values and opinions. As teachers we can be aware of this bias and try to manage it, but it is very difficult not to treat likable students differently, for example, by spending more time with them during advising. These are the students who are more likely to be invited for coffee.

The ethical stand is clear when preferences are based on gender or ethnicity. Prejudice is wrong, but often it is subtle. Do we pay more attention to the men than the women in our class? Do we ignore foreign students by not finding out how to involve them in class discussions?

Are some faculty unintentionally racist? Faculty may be unaware of the biases they show in class, but unintended racism is no more ethical than intentional racism.

In presenting these issues it is not my intent to discuss them specifically, but to show that there are many aspects of teaching to which ethical principles may be applied, and that it is important for teachers to think about how they would deal with such issues should they encounter them.

Some ethical issues relate to teacher performance more than to our relationships with students. Consider our responsibility to provide students with good academic content and to deliver it effectively. There are some teachers whose content is out of date, whose presentation is disorganized, and whose lectures are delivered in a monotone. Isn't that unethical? How bad does teaching have to get before it is unethical?

Consider a teacher who may frequently be absent from class. The ethical problem is different depending on whether the absence is due to serious illness, or to alcohol abuse, or to conflicting demands from other professional responsibilities. I think we would agree that we should help our colleague who is ill, but what about the other two cases? Perhaps the most difficult ethical dilemma for teachers concerns the conditions under which we should take action and what actions to take. When should we seek help for an alcoholic colleague or report an absentee traveler to our dean or impose "faculty development" on a boring teacher? Almost any attempt to take action against a perceived wrong will take a great deal of time and may involve risk to one's own career, so most teachers are reluctant to take that step. This brings to mind one of my favorite quotations from Mark Twain: "To be good is noble, but to teach others to be good is nobler—and less trouble."

When making ethical decisions for one's self or when considering the actions of others it might help to have some guidelines, such as we have for some professions. The American Association of University Professors (AAUP) adopted a statement on professional ethics in 1966 and endorsed it again in 1987. It contains five paragraphs on different aspects of academic life, the second of which concerns teaching:

> As teachers, professors encourage the free pursuit of learning in their students. They hold before them the best scholarly and ethical standards of their discipline. Professors demonstrate respect for students as individuals and adhere to their proper roles as intellectual guides and counselors. Professors make every reasonable effort to foster honest academic conduct and

to ensure that their evaluations of students reflect each student's true merit. They respect the confidential nature of the relationship between professor and student. They avoid any exploitation, harassment, or discriminatory treatment of students. They acknowledge significant academic or scholarly assistance from them. They protect their academic freedom.[2]

This statement provides some guidance in a general way, but it still leaves many ambiguous situations, and that is the nature of ethical judgment. This makes it even more important for us to consider our own individual ethical positions and to expect that graduate students who are planning on an academic career develop their own philosophy of teaching.

Teaching the Ethics of Teaching

In my course on the teaching of psychology we devote at least two class periods specifically to the topic of ethics. The primary method that I use is to first ask students to examine their own experiences with teachers who have been unethical and then to look at selected cases that represent some of the issues I have raised. Part of our analysis of each case is a discussion of what we would have done if we were the teacher in that case.

However, I do not advocate an approach that is entirely case-based. I think we should become aware of the ethical principles that we are applying in considering these cases, and these principles should become part of our philosophy of teaching. The development of a philosophy of teaching is a major feature of my course, and of the certificate program and portfolio workshops offered by our teaching center.

Philosophy statements usually are about two pages long, and written in the first person using nontechnical language. Most philosophies will say something about beliefs and values, an idea of teaching excellence or of the ideal teacher, and a view of how people learn. It is likely that words or phrases will be included in this statement that are related to ethical principles. Here is an example from a philosophy statement that appeared in one portfolio (my own) submitted to our certificate program:

Teaching is a form of service to others, my students. It often is defined as the facilitation of learning, but for me it also means helping students develop as persons. My task as a teacher is to educate the whole person, and to do this by words and examples. I respect students as free, responsible individuals, whose most important task is learning how to learn. Classes, assignments and other requirements may help with this process, but should not interfere with it.

Here we see at least two basic ethical principles: beneficence (wanting to help) and autonomy or respect for persons (respecting students as free, responsible individuals). We would expect to see these principles reflected in this teacher's classes, in how he relates to students, meets his obligations and is available, and provides opportunities for choice in the context of course requirements.

Making one's teaching philosophy explicit in this way provides an occasion for interesting discussions with colleagues. How much help should you give students and in what ways? Should we never harm students, for example, by giving them a failing grade? How much freedom is compatible with an obligation to help students?

Another important ethical principle is that of justice. Like cases should be treated alike, that is, equals treated equally and unequals treated unequally. However, philosophers ask, what are the criteria for equality? We might consider effort, merit, equal access, or need. Teachers struggle with this particularly when assigning grades, where merit usually is assumed to be the criterion, but where other factors may enter given the amount of subjectivity in the grading process.

This is the most important ethical issue for students according to a survey published several years ago.[3] They want teachers to be fair and see bias as the most common ethical violation by teachers. We might respond that it is only the students who get lower grades than expected who think we are not fair, but I believe we should try to consider ways in which we might unintentionally be unjust. I may be posing problems or using language that students from another culture do not understand. My wish to help some students may cause me to ignore others who are less assertive in seeking help.   Perhaps we have an obligation to determine student perceptions of justice in our classes.

The Teacher as Exemplar of Virtue

Recently much has been written about the academic honesty and integrity of students. We are upset by student cheating on examinations and by students who submit papers that have been copied or purchased. There have been disturbing reports of extreme incivility by students toward faculty, including physical as well as verbal assaults. Tolerance also is a problem, both lack of tolerance for others, as seen in reports of racist attacks, as well as willingness to tolerate the crimes of society. We have an obligation to confront these issues when they occur, and to try to prevent them from occurring, which is one objective of teaching ethics across the curriculum.

It is less likely that students will be ethical if they perceive us, their teachers, to be unethical or to see ethics as not our concern. One place to develop that concern is with conversations among ourselves about the difficult ethical issues that we face and about the ethical principles that are part of our personal philosophy of teaching. Included in those conversations should be the next generation of teachers, our graduate students and the newer members of our community. To the extent that the Center for Teaching Excellence can promote these discussions, it will have fulfilled an important part of its mission.

Notes

[1] Barbara G. Tabachnick, Patricia C. Keith-Spiegel, and Kenneth S. Pope, "Ethics of Teaching: Beliefs and Behaviors of Psychologists as Educators," *American Psychologist* 46 (1991): 506–515.

[2] The complete statement can be found on the AAUP web site: http://www.aaup. org/Rbethics.htm.

[3] Patricia C. Keith-Spiegel, Barbara G. Tabachnick, and M. Allen, "Ethics in Academia: Students' Views of Professors' Actions," *Ethics and Behavior* 3 (1993): 149–162.

ETHICS IS AN OPTICS

Michael D. Barber, S.J.
Department of Philosophy

To appreciate the importance of ethics for my discipline—philosophy—we need to return to our lived experiences of each other before we ever begin to do philosophy or to theorize. A careful phenomenological description of how the other person is given would reveal the Other as one who summons us to an ethical response in his or her presence.

I enter a room and discover a total stranger there and I acknowledge her presence, "Good morning," and in reflecting I become aware that the other person evoked that greeting, that there was a claim on me for recognition; in my response, I discover the other's call. Or consider a person confronting me on the street asking for money. Suddenly I find myself drawn up short before this other person, fumbling for change or, fearing that this is a con-game, trying to figure out what to say, or perhaps I cross the street because I know that when my eyes meet the beggar's eyes an appeal will be addressed to me to which I will have to reply in some way. Or examine what is going on now between us. As I speak, you are paying attention to what I say, striving to understand, evaluating or readying a responsible critique, and this very seriousness with which you take me is an act of ethical service on your part; you honor me in response to something in me that invites that response. Similarly, in my laboring on this talk, working to present it clearly, attending to your facial expressions, to your looks of agreement or disagreement or confusion, I find myself offering you service that you are evoking from me.

While these examples make focal the ethical dimensions of relationships, I cannot imagine any face-to-face relationship, such as economic, sexual, or political, devoid of such dimensions even if they are not always made explicit. The pedagogical relationship, with which we are all acquainted, is ethically saturated, as students solicit our responsiveness and efforts to assist them in developing the knowledge and formation they will need when they leave us. Finally, even though ethical obligations become visible paradigmatically in the face-to-face, the Other not physically or temporally proximate still has an ethical claim upon us.

A more careful analysis of this experience of the Other would show, I think, that I do not create the ethical summons issuing from you out of my own resources, from my own background, although my cultural and religious background no doubt helps me to recognize the summons. Furthermore, the existence of these ethical mandates given in the face of the Other and disclosed in our careful reflection is not disproved by the abundant empirical evidence, particularly in the twentieth century, that many or even the majority may have ignored or run roughshod over these mandates. Ethical resistance is the resistance that has no resistance, no physical power, it is often at its strongest in destitution, and it is not snuffed out even when the Other is murdered insofar as the eyes of Abel still stare at Cain from the grave.

Given this account of ethical relationships at the pretheoretical level, what happens when one embarks upon a theorizing activity? First of all, theorizing is but one of several possible responses to the Other. When speaking with a grieving friend, for instance, an ethically more appropriate response might be to hold silently the friend's hand rather than to launch into one's latest theory about the stages of grieving. But on other occasions, one's interlocutor requests the response of theory by raising a question or making a claim. Once again, we usually jump into theoretical discourse with each other without being aware that there is anything ethical about it at all or that this discourse answers to another's bidding. Thus we resemble the creation in Genesis that came into being, responding so quickly and without self-consciousness upon hearing God's command that we easily forget that in the beginning there wasn't even anything there to do the hearing or the obeying. In this light, one who attends carefully to what goes on in academic conferences in every discipline will uncover impressive ethical dimensions. To develop a full and responsible account of one's own position and present it to others, to listen carefully and critically and present the fairest, most balanced criticism one can muster—all this is to behave with ethical reverence for an interlocutor. Conversely, we find ethically offensive the dogmatic refusal to discuss, the *ad hominem*, or the deliberate caricature of an opponent. This account of the pretheoretical ethical relationship becomes a kind of optics—ethics is an optics—with which to view what we might have thought were purely theoretical exchanges devoid of any ethical features.

Philosophy, as one theoretical domain among others, has its own theoretical subdivisions: theory of knowledge, philosophy of religion, philosophy of science, philosophy of human nature, ethics—but insofar as all these subdivisions involve theory and discourse, one person making and justifying claims to another, ethical dimensions are unavoidable. As a result, Emmanuel Levinas, on whose theory I am relying heavily here, states that morality is not a branch of philosophy, but first philosophy. There is also something unavoidable and "foundational" about these ethical dimensions because even those who come forward to dispute these ethical dimensions enjoin us take them seriously, to listen to their arguments, and to develop responsible replies. They presuppose the very ethical dimensions they dispute. The inescapability of these ethical dimensions of discourse, taken as a kind of foundation, gives no grounds for arrogance or dogmatism, though, since placed before the Other, one is exposed to contestation, drawn into a discussion whose outcome is unpredictable and uncertain, far from any unfolding of a "prefabricated internal logic."

While the diverse philosophical regions all depend upon discourse, they nevertheless have their own autonomy, their own distinctive problems, vocabularies, and usually long histories of discussion with which a responsible interlocutor must deal. Ethical theory, for instance, usually begins with everyday ethical claims and considers whether or how those claims can be justified to an inquiring discourse partner. Ethical theory explores the differences and relations between normative and factual discourses, between ethics and science. It argues within the context of moral-practical rationality for first principles by which one might validate or invalidate ethical claims, and it explores the role of virtues in relation to principles. While the relationship to the Other underpins this discourse, the various arguments must be examined and criticized in their own terms—are they valid? consistent? sufficiently comprehensive? etc. However, one's ethical commitment to the Other might serve as a touchstone for one's ethical theory. One would feel something amiss about a theory whose tendencies might be to de-emphasize the Other's worth, and such feeling would prompt a theoretical response, which, of course, must engage critically the interlocutor's validity claims in their terms and in their subtlety.

In addition, starting with the pretheoretical relationship with the Other, with this ethics as an optics, it is possible to envision the problems addressed within traditional philosophical domains in a new light. For instance, criticisms of epistemological relativism have generally been pursued in terms of whether the practices of the natural sciences could ever countenance relativism or whether the translation that actually takes place across supposedly incommensurable frameworks really disproves total relativism, etc. However, epistemological relativism would appear in a new perspective considered through the optics of ethics. Epistemological relativism, crudely expressed in one of its least defensible forms as "everyone has their own incommensurable worldviews and there can be no truth beyond such worldviews," involves a kind of self-enclosure within worldviews that shuts the other person or culture out. Convinced that worldviews are self-enclosed, epistemological relativists can refuse to submit their own views to testing by the Other whose relative worldview has no more purchase on the truth than their own. Epistemological relativism can thereby preclude the possibility of learning from the Other and can render futile any search for truth between cultures in ethical solidarity.

Or how might one approach the problem of evil in the philosophy of religion through the optics of ethics? Given the massive horror of the Holocaust whose victims still forbid us to forget, it becomes ethically problematic to tell victims in the midst of their suffering that through their suffering God is achieving divine purposes unbeknown to them. The whole problem of evil, though, originates not in cynicism but in ethical outrage about innocent suffering that seems irreconcilable with an ethical God, and one's desire for ethical integrity demands that one think through the problem. The book of Job then paints a sublime picture of this struggle for ethical integrity, with Job's protest of unfairness and God's willingness to enter humbly into dialogue with Job revealing the ethicality of Job, God, and the author of the book of Job. If ethics is an optics through which to approach the varied spheres of philosophy, it is also an optics through which one can read the classical literature of the history of philosophy. It opens up a vast and novel way for the future study of philosophy.

In like vein, the relationship with the excluded, forgotten, or misunderstood Other functions as an optics from which to write history, study literature, or carry on one's discipline. Here the pretheoretical ethics elaborated above can support in interdisciplinary fashion attempts to rewrite the history written by the victors and neglecting the vanquished, to recover great literary voices once mistakenly deemed insignificant, or to ensure that one's theology or one's economics not be indifferent toward those enduring worldwide the scourge of poverty or malnutrition. In all these endeavors, one is not just studying history, literature, theology, or economics—one is also responding ethically to an Other, perhaps distant, perhaps long deceased, whose plea for recognition and justice still persists.

But you might be thinking, we have heard much about ethics and the other, but what about the self? What about reciprocal relationships and equality? What about the evil other whom one ought to fear rather than serve? First of all, ethics is an optics from which to view the constitution of the self. To speak of loving myself is to relate to myself as if I were another, is to transfer the respect and reverence learned in relationship with the other person to myself. Certainly also healthy self-love constitutes a condition of loving others generously, authentically, and faithfully. But why are we tempted to think that there is opposition between service of the Other and strength of self? Think of the young man who becomes a father for the first time and his new child focuses his energies and perhaps for the first time he acquires an identity as someone with a responsibility he cannot shirk. Even more so, think of Archbishop Romero of El Salvador, at first a timid, fearful cleric; but more and more haunted by the slaughter of innocent peasants in the countryside, he stood up courageously without any protection against huge forces arrayed against him. Because he was more concerned about the murder of others rather than his own death—a complete reversal of the existentialist creed—he had nothing to lose, he was a fearless self. In the optics of ethics, service does not diminish the self but makes it.

If I am to myself an Other deserving reverence like all Others, then the equality and reciprocity that all major ethical theories insist on is a requisite here too. Service to the Other does not require that one accept abuse from the Other, not only for one's own sake, but also for the Other. One does not respect the Other by allowing him or her to treat others unequally, without reciprocity, to act without being held accountable. Similarly, it is important to call citizens to responsibility for their society, not to take advantage of it as free-riders, but not principally because one resents taxes being paid to pick up the tab, but because it is not good for them to be unaccountable or irresponsible. If an ethical relationship of solidarity underlies all efforts to help people grow into reciprocity and responsibility—to be responsible for even their responsibility—then even if they fail to live up to standards of reciprocity, we will not be permitted to stop trying or to abandon them. Finally, there is indeed the dangerous other, not to be naively trusted, the criminal prowling the street, the enemy armed and dangerous. But if there isn't some appeal for mercy even in the face of the enemy or the criminal, why is it that soldiers must undergo extensive training so as not to feel any compassion for the enemy? Why the nightmares long after the war is over? Why have several executioners so no one of them will know who threw the switch, shot the bullet, or dropped the pellet? Why the sense of tragedy, the regret that no communication was possible when the thief was shot down in the street? Through the optics of ethics, coercion, even justified coercion, happens against the background of the Other who faces us ethically.

But the possibility of war reveals also how ethics as traditionally understood can be dangerous. One can become convinced of the rightness of one's cause, buttress convictions with elaborate defenses, and in the name of this rightness inflict violence upon others. And yet such violence doesn't even seem to be violence so self-justified is it, so shrouded in the mantle of virtue. In the twentieth century we have witnessed repeatedly the horror that this dynamic produces and present-day global confrontations forebode more of the same. Think of the different ethnic groups squaring off in the Balkans or the secularized West bearing its standards of democracy and modernization facing off an Islam bent on preserving age-old religious traditions. Of course, one can adopt a Nietzschean anti-ethics and discredit all ethics and reason as mere extensions of power, all the more dangerous for concealing that power behind a veneer of goodness and truth. But one can also find in the face of the Other an anti-ethics that pleads against violence, that raises questions even about ethical codes and theoretical justifications, that invites to conversation, humility, patience, and mutual learning. This is an anti-ethics that is really profoundly pro-ethics, that is, it is an anti-ethics for the sake of authentic ethics.

Hence, exposure to the face of the Other is a route to authentic ethics. But the dangers of traditional ethics also imperil the traditional search for truth. We can convince ourselves of our reasons, elaborate our defenses, wrap ourselves in the mantle of truth, and set off to wage war. Given this possibility, exposure to the face of the Other is also the route to authentic truth; it is an optics through which we can come to recognize the wisdom that philosophy has always loved.

THREE ESSENTIALS IN UNDERGRADUATE EDUCATION

Mark Chmiel
Department of Theological Studies

I remember as I began teaching as an adjunct here at Saint Louis University four semesters ago, I came across some challenging advice from the sociologist Alan Wolfe. After many years of teaching, Wolfe was convinced that undergraduates today needed nurturance in developing three areas of their lives: first, a sense of wonder and awe; second, a tragic sense of life; and third, a code of ethics.

I would like to reflect with you about these three aims in the context of my teaching an upper-division course called Social Justice in the Department of Theological Studies.

First, on cultivating students' sense of wonder and awe. When I began planning this course, I realized that one option would be to focus on issues such as the growing gap between the rich and the poor, ecological destruction, or the global arms trade. Another option would be to study some of the major documents of the Catholic tradition on social justice. But rather than go in these directions, I had a hunch that students might value exposure to some role models in social justice. So I shaped the course, for the most part, around biography, how people grew into a commitment to social justice. In informal exchanges with some students, I've noticed some not surprising language they use at this Jesuit university: they are mindful of their "formation" in their four years here. Some take seriously the official Jesuit discourse about becoming men and women for others. They already experience how the culture at large is forming them in particular ways; however, some of them hope for a specific Christian formation. I believed that for students like these—who are open, questioning, and committed—a biographical focus in social justice would speak to some of their own personal questions in a way that hard analysis of depressing issues might not.

We have studied biographies and autobiographies of people like the Hindu practitioner of nonviolence, Mohandas Gandhi; the co-founder of the Catholic Worker, Dorothy Day; the Buddhist leader in the Vietnamese peace movement, Sister Chân Không; the Jesuit rector of the Central American University, Ignacio Ellacuria, murdered in El Salvador in 1989; Martin Luther King, Jr. and Malcolm X, African-American leaders in the struggle against white supremacy, to name some of them.[1]

At some point late in the semester, I usually pose this question to the students: "Which of the men and women we have studied most captures your imagination?" Many say Dorothy Day. They are intrigued by her youthful experimentation, her various love affairs, her daring independence, and her abortion, and they are amazed at how far she went after her conversion to Catholicism when she devoted the rest of her life to serving the poor and resisting what she called "this filthy, rotten system" of American capitalism.[2] Other students are mesmerized by Gandhi, who tried to assimilate to British customs before devoting his life to the systematic practice of nonviolence in thought, word, and deed as a way of life and practical strategy for resolving conflict. Still other students are fascinated to learn of the difficult journey of Malcolm X who had typically—and briefly—been described as an extremist in their high school history classes, but who captivates the students because of his fearlessness and truth-telling.

I should note that our treatment is not pious hagiography. What the students seem grateful for is the candid portrayal of the earthiness, the wandering, the mistakes of people with whom they can identify. These 20-year-olds seem to have an acute sense of human imperfection, beginning when they look in the mirror. What these students so often express is what Wolfe termed awe and wonder—the students learn how these ordinary people became extraordinary. They see that Gandhi was an utterly uninspiring young person who through spiritual discipline transformed himself to become a leader for Indian independence, and they have an inkling that a life of service is possible for them, too. They believe Gandhi when he said, "I have not the shadow of a doubt that any man or woman can achieve what I have, if he or she would make the same effort and cultivate the same hope and faith."[3] Their awe for Gandhi is also an awe for their own "coming into focus" capacities.

In addition to this study of such people, it is always a highlight when I invite former Saint Louis University students to testify about their own work in social justice. The current students are both inspired and challenged by the commitment of their own peers, and they begin to ask, "If they can do such things, why can't I?" Or, "Why aren't I?"

Second, on fostering a tragic sense of life. Some of the students in the course have confessed: "I leave our class every Tuesday and Thursday with such a heavy heart." I try to encourage them: "I would be worried if you didn't."

Through the life stories, we sharpen our awareness of the injustice and suffering in the world that seems of an entirely different order than the parking problems, tenure pressures, and dateless Friday nights of Saint Louis University. We see how the men and women in their communities faced and fought against such pervasive injustices as colonialism, poverty, racism, and war. Many of the students lose their political and social innocence in this class.

For example, as we investigate the life and work of Maryknoll missionary Roy Bourgeois, students learn about the United States Army School of the Americas, which has trained Latin American soldiers and officers for many years in terror and torture tactics.[4] Many students become outraged when they discover this school's link to the assassins of the Salvadoran Jesuits in 1989, the four United States churchwomen and Archbishop Oscar Romero in 1980, plus thousands of unnamed union organizers, catechists, teachers, and other civilians throughout Latin America. They are aghast that their United States tax dollars help fund this school and that United States practice is so at odds with United States government rhetoric.

Studying and processing these matters through small- and large-group discussions may lead some students to experience a heavy heart. Then, there are some other students who make a weekly volunteer commitment and devote their spring break to immersion experiences offered through Campus Ministry. It is here that students can have their hearts broken.[5] Whether it is on Native American reservations, the Texas-Mexican border, or urban shelters, some students correlate what they are reading with their own experiences of profound compassion as they see for themselves that there is an aching world beyond their relative comfort zone of a statue- and palm-tree-laden campus. They confront what the Church calls "social sin" and are initially overwhelmed by its magnitude. Moreover, they begin to understand that so much suffering is unnecessary, and is the result of institutions which value profit, power, and prestige over human dignity.

Third, on nurturing an ethical code. Each of the people we study in this course attempted to follow a particularly rigorous ethics of personal and social transformation. Students learn how these women and men followed a set of practices which often demanded civic courage, nonviolent discipline, and solidarity with those suffering. Moreover, through the life stories of these women and men, students see how they made changes in their lives, how they were converted, how they struggled, how they sacrificed.

From Dorothy Day, we learn about the practice of the corporal and spiritual works of mercy and from Maryknoll Father Roy Bourgeois we learn about the preferential option for the poor. But I also quite consciously choose people outside the Catholic tradition; for example, from Gandhi we learn about *ahimsa*, or nonharming and the various ways Gandhi transformed his anger into compassionate energy to struggle for social change. From Chân Không, we learn about the 14 precepts she and other Buddhists followed as they tried to unite the traditional Buddhist practice of mindfulness with service to their people who were being bombed and tortured during the Vietnam War. One of these precepts—which all of the figures in the course embody in one way or another—reads as follows: "Do not avoid contact with suffering or close your eyes before suffering. Do not lose awareness of the existence of suffering in the life of the world. Find ways to be with those who are suffering, including personal contact, visits, images, and sounds. By such means, awaken yourself and others to the reality of suffering in the world."[6]

It's one thing for their elders to insist that younger people follow a demanding ethical code. It is another thing to learn of someone like Chân Không living it out, in the most severe conditions, with a serenity that is both amazing and convincing.

There are two sides to embracing such an ethical code of practices, attitudes, and values, what the scholars call the hermeneutics of suspicion and generosity, or critique and fidelity toward one's religious tradition. Students are impressed that Gandhi opposed the Indian caste system; they are invigorated by Dorothy Day's calling to account the rich Catholics who prided themselves on their charity but who were oblivious to the demands of justice. They identify with Chân Không who was frustrated by Buddhist teachers who emphasized meditation to the exclusion of relieving the suffering right before them. But the students also see how these men and women retrieved and lived out key teachings and found great sustenance in their respective Scriptures, spiritual disciplines such as prayer and fasting, and communal celebration.

To conclude, as I have spent the last week in reading course projects and final exams, I am reminded by student reflections of three themes that speak to them in this course.

First is the example of the lives of men and women for others. Our subjects remind students that there's more to life than public conquests and private consumption. Their own journeys awaken in our students the moral motivation to embark upon a new way of life.

A second theme is the valuable resources of the world's religious traditions to address some of our global problems—students become ecumenically sensitive as they realize that no one religious tradition has a monopoly on ethical wisdom but that there's a lot in their own tradition that they can apply. Many Christians throughout the twentieth century have testified that it took a Hindu like Gandhi to teach them the power and practicality of Jesus' Sermon on the Mount.

And third is the necessity of religious self-criticism—students realize that some of the great religious leaders of the twentieth century have been adamant critics as well of their own traditions in this cause of social justice. The bumper-sticker imperative "Question authority" acquires a depth and immediacy from the witness of these men and women, so often misunderstood by their own co-religionists and contemporaries.

A final comment about modesty. Early last fall, I had a sobering yet illuminating conversation with a former student. He was one of those who took immediately to the course in social justice; he is a campus leader, a very fine student, a volunteer at the Catholic worker shelter. He said matter of factly, "Most teachers really have no idea what's going on in the lives of their students. Often, the classroom is the last place that students have really important learning experiences." I swallowed hard, utterly naive: "Really?" I have learned a lot since that encounter.

If what this student avers is even partially true, then it may be that we need to have a day devoted to "Ethics Across the University" when faculty could get to listen to presentations by students from whom we might learn a great deal. After that, I suspect a day or two on "Ethics Across Midtown" might even be appropriate where we might all listen to what our neighbors have to say to us about ethics.

Notes

[1] See Eknath Easwaran, *Gandhi The Man: The Story of His Transformation* (Tomales, CA: Nilgiri Press, 1997); Jim Forest, *Love Is the Measure: A Biography of Dorothy Day*, rev. ed. (Maryknoll, NY: Orbis Books, 1994); Chân Không, *Learning True Love: How I Learned and Practiced Social Change in Vietnam* (Berkeley: Parallax Press, 1993); Jon Sobrino, Ignacio Ellacuria et al., *Companions of Jesus: The Jesuit Martyrs of El Salvador* (Maryknoll, NY: Orbis Books, 1990); and James H. Cone, *Martin & Malcolm & America: A Dream or a Nightmare* (Maryknoll, NY: Orbis Books, 1991).

[2] Forest, *Love Is the Measure*, 123.
[3] Quoted in Easwaran, *Gandhi the Man*, 1.
[4] See Jack Nelson-Pallmeyer, *School of Assassins: The Case for Closing the School of the Americas and for Fundamentally Changing United States Foreign Policy* (Maryknoll, NY: Orbis Books, 1997).
[5] For more on the necessary experience of the poor breaking our hearts, see Dean Brackley, S.J., *The Christian University and Liberation: The Challenge of the UCA* (St. Louis, MO: The Institute of Jesuit Sources, 1992), 14–15.
[6] Quoted in Chân Không, *Learning True Love*, 80.

ATTENTION TO VULNERABILITY AS A CONDITION FOR A UNIVERSITY COMMUNITY COMMITTED TO ETHICAL TREATMENT OF OTHERS

Judith L. Gibbons
Department of Psychology

My discipline is developmental psychology; specifically I study the development of adolescents who are growing up in different cultural settings. Developmental psychology attends to differences among individuals of different ages that occur because of changes in developmental tasks that people face over the life span. Ross Thompson has elaborated one way that developmental psychologists might contribute to the ethics of psychological research.[1] Developmental psychologists can pay attention to how age, developmental stage, or social condition that is associated with a developmental stage may lead to particular kinds of vulnerability in research. For example, Thompson describes the vulnerability of young children to separation from their parents and the vulnerability of teenagers to threats to their self-esteem. A 12-month old toddler left in the company of strangers in a research situation might feel distress and begin to cry. A teenager is not likely to feel distressed by a 15-minute separation from her mother, but she might feel disturbed by a questionnaire which asks about her breast development, or by rumors that her classmates had listed her as the peer they would least like to work with.

What I would like to do is extend the concept of developmental vulnerability to university students, and then, briefly, describe how developmental vulnerability might apply to other members of the university community. In what ways are the persons we see every day —especially students, but also other faculty and staff—vulnerable because of the developmental tasks they face or the social conditions associated with those tasks? What, specifically, are the vulnerabilities? Are there ways to acknowledge, lessen, or counteract the risks?

The typical college-age person (ages 18 to 25) is at the stage of late adolescence. During this period in life certain risky behaviors reach their height.[2] This is the peak stage for driving at high speeds, especially while drinking, and the rates of automobile accidents are higher among late adolescents than for any other age group. During late adolescence and early adulthood, risky sexual behavior also reaches its height, resulting in higher rates of sexually transmitted diseases than at other ages. College-age persons are at risk for substance abuse, especially alcohol, and alcohol may contribute to other risky behaviors. Delinquency and crime are also at their peak during the late adolescent and early adult years.[3] Although not many students at Saint Louis University are likely to be involved in criminal behavior, it is likely that exposure to the risky behaviors of their cohort might seep into their thinking and choices, and create a milieu in which danger and crime seem routine and unremarkable. Studies of risk-taking among adolescents have shown that many teenagers consider risk-taking to be normative; taking risks is necessary to gain life experiences, and will be outgrown as the teenagers become adults.[4] My students tell me that what they would consider normative for their peers—for example, to get extremely drunk at a party—they would consider to be symptomatic of problems in a person of my generation.

Late adolescents and young adults are also vulnerable in other ways. Although loneliness is associated with the stereotype of older adults, in fact, college-age persons, particularly freshmen, show the highest levels of loneliness, isolation, and feelings of lonesomeness than any other age group.[5] Although depression is not at its peak, about one of four university students shows a clinically significant level of depression. Women who are college students are three times as likely to be victims of rape and sexual assault, particularly acquaintance rape, than other women.[6] College-age women are also at high risk for eating disorders. A recent study showed that two-thirds of university students had experienced a traumatic event, most often a natural disaster, but also other traumas such as a serious accident, physical and sexual abuse, or physical assault.[7] Women, more often than men, had experienced sexual coercion or assault, whereas men had more often suffered a serious accident or physical assault.[8] As a teacher, the high incidence of trauma has become evident to me in my course on the psychology of women, a course in which, each semester, students tell me about their personal experiences with sexual abuse, battering, and rape.

The daily normative stressors of college students also affect their well-being.[9] There is some evidence that daily hassles lead to depression to a greater extent than do major traumas, perhaps because individuals receive more social support for trauma than for the hassles of everyday life.[10] The everyday stresses of university students include pressure to succeed in their classes, to get into graduate or medical school, and to make career decisions. The biggest pressures surround school work itself—how to do well, including understanding the content, doing the readings, completing all the assignments on time, and passing the tests. According to Erikson, the major developmental task of young adulthood is achieving intimacy in close relationships, including both friendships and romantic relationships.[11] The everyday stressors related to forming and maintaining friendships and romantic relationships significantly affect college students' well-being and happiness.

Related to the pressures of school work and relationships are those of money and finances. If students don't do well in classes, they lose their financial aid, and then will have to work at paid jobs for more hours. Working for many hours further decreases their ability to devote time to school work, which leads their grades to suffer even more. Relationships also suffer from lack of time. Time and time management as related to money, school work, relationships, and work at a job are major stressors for many students. They feel especially disadvantaged by assignments that they perceive as busywork, or frivolous, designed merely to take up time, rather than lead to significant learning.

In terms of class work and assignments, university students may be particularly vulnerable because of limited social power.[12] It is the professors who design the curriculum, choose the textbooks, make the assignments, and make decisions about the class structure and content. So, in at least one domain which is already full of stresses, students may suffer additionally from restricted ability to exert influence.

Moreover, some groups of students might be particularly vulnerable. For example, students whose first language is not English may be worried about oral presentations in class. Ethnic minority students often feel pressure from increased visibility and may worry that the teacher will notice if they are absent or tardy. Students with disabilities continue to suffer from negative stereotypes.[13] Gay and lesbian students are often the "invisible minority" and may suffer from heterosexist assumptions implicit in some course materials. One of the unaddressed issues in university education is that of social class and hidden classism. In a study of elementary schools, middle-class teachers perceived low-income children as lazy, rebellious, and fun-loving, whereas teachers who were themselves from low-income backgrounds saw the same children as happy, cooperative, and energetic.[14] A study of high school students showed that a feeling of not fitting in was a mediator of lower grades among low-income students.[15]

How might we, as faculty respond to the vulnerability and developmental risks of the students in our classes? A good beginning would be to acknowledge vulnerabilities, especially hidden ones, and to express solidarity with those who have experienced trauma and who experience loneliness. For example, in psychology of women, I point out the statistics on the prevalence of acquaintance rape, and the likelihood that members of the class have been victims. Then, rather than always saying "they," I sometimes use the pronoun "we" to refer to victims of violence against women. Secondly, I think that we might better design assignments to directly combat loneliness that may arise not only from the developmental tasks of late adolescence, but also from the experience of living away from home for the first time, as well as the legacy of living in the most individualistic country in the world. Those assignments might be especially useful for freshmen and might involve working in teams or groups so that students might get to know each other, and not feel so alone in doing their assignments. In the psychology of women, I offer the option of writing a paper on one's mother's life. This accomplishes both the purpose of finding out about one woman's life, and also (usually) increases feelings of closeness of the student and his/her mother.

Additionally, I'd like to extend the notion of vulnerability to other members of the university community. How might staff members be vulnerable because of their social condition and developmental tasks? According to Erikson, during middle adulthood individuals strive for generativity—contributing something of value to the next generation.[16] Generativity may be expressed in a variety of ways, from raising children to making a contribution through a job or occupation. Staff members might find their generativity blocked if their contribution to the university was thwarted or not adequately acknowledged. Women, particularly, might feel stress from the simultaneous demands of family and job. Another vulnerability of staff members comes from their economic dependence on the university. Anything that threatens their job in any way would generally leave staff members feeling vulnerable.

What about other constituencies? Faculty, for the most part, face developmental tasks that are similar to those of staff. A major concern of faculty members is generativity, how to make a significant contribution to society and subsequent generations. Moreover, the various domains of generativity may compete for time and resources, with faculty experiencing vulnerability on various fronts, including conflicts between family time and professional commitments, and competing demands of scholarship and teaching. Like students, particular groups of faculty may be at special risk. Tenure-track faculty may feel extremely vulnerable in the university, imperiled by requirements for simultaneous excellence in all areas—scholarship, teaching, advising, service, and collegiality. Faculty on the verge of retirement may have additional vulnerabilities. In his theory of development Erikson proposed that older individuals experience well-being and satisfaction from having left behind a legacy.[17] For senior faculty rapid transformations of their areas of scholarship, elimination of curricula or programs they had implemented, or other vast changes might undermine their satisfaction in having made a contribution to succeeding generations.

Finally, we might note the ways in which developmental vulnerabilities might intersect. Like parents, faculty may have a "generational stake" in seeing their ideas continued into the next generation. Students, on the other hand, are looking forward to the future, in terms of initiating careers and establishing relationships as couples and future families. The implications of the different points of view of students and faculty remain unexplored.

In conclusion, Thompson's notion of developmental vulnerability can be applied to the situation of the university community. One way that developmental psychologists can make a contribution toward creating an ethos of ethics in the university is by highlighting and underscoring developmental issues that lead individuals to experience areas of vulnerability. The areas of vulnerability differ for persons of different ages and roles at the university. Students who are young adults, the age of most Saint Louis University students, are vulnerable to loneliness, trauma, accidents, and alcohol abuse. They also experience daily stressors which, though normative, can exacerbate or precipitate other problems. A preliminary glimpse at issues that affect other members of the university community, including faculty and staff, suggests that they, too, may be vulnerable because of the developmental tasks they face. Staff members may be vulnerable to insufficient opportunity to use their skills, junior faculty may suffer risks related to tenure evaluation, and senior faculty may be concerned about their lifetime contribution to the discipline and to the university.

The first step in addressing issues of vulnerability within the university community is to identify them and to understand how they might serve to influence teaching and learning. A second step is to design interventions that lessen or counteract the risks. Although a few suggestions have been offered, it is incumbent on all of us as a community to come up with strategies that account for vulnerabilities and reduce risk as part of our respect for persons. By attending to developmental issues we can further the development of a university community based on an ethos of ethics.

Author's note

The author would like to thank Janet Kuebli and James Korn for their careful reading of an earlier version of the manuscript and the Beaumont Faculty Development Fund for support for scholarship endeavors. Judith Gibbons may be reached by e-mail at: gibbonsj1@slu.edu.

Notes

[1] Ross A. Thompson, "Vulnerability in Research: A Developmental Perspective on Research Risk," *Child Development* 61 (1990): 1–16.

[2] J. J. Arnett, "Adolescent Storm and Stress, Reconsidered," *American Psychologist* (in press).

[3] Ibid.

[4] Cynthia Lightfoot, *The Culture of Adolescent Risk Taking* (New York: Guilford Press, 1997).

[5] Carolyn E. Cutrona, "Transition to College: Loneliness and the Process of Social Adjustment," in *Loneliness: A Sourcebook of Current Theory, Research, and Therapy*, ed. Letita Anne Peplau and Daniel Perlman (New York: Wiley, 1982): 291–309.

[6] Marta Aizenman and Georgette Kelley, "The Incidence of Violence and Acquaintance Rape in Dating Relationships Among College Men and Women," *Journal of College Student Development* 29 (1988): 305–311.

[7] Jeffrey A. Bernat, Heidi M. Ronfeldt, Karen S. Calhoun, and Ileana Arias, "Prevalence of Traumatic Events and Peritraumatic Predictors of Posttraumatic Stress Symptoms in a Nonclinical Sample of College Students," *Journal of Traumatic Stress* 11 (1998): 645–664.

[8] Ibid.

[9] James H. Brooks and David L. DuBois, "Individual and Environmental Predictors of Adjustment During the First Year of College," *Journal of College Student Development* 36 (1995): 347–360.

[10] Gordon L. Flett, Kirk R. Blankstein, D. Janine Hicken, and Mark S. Watson, "Social Support and Help-Seeking in Daily Hassles versus Major Life Events Stress," *Journal of Applied Social Psychology* 25 (1995): 49–58.

[11] Erik H. Erikson, *Adulthood* (New York: W.W. Norton, 1978).

[12] See Ross A. Thompson, "Vulnerability in Research: A Developmental Perspective on Research Risk," for the implications for children.

[13] Cristina Cambra, "A Comparative Study of Personality Descriptors Attributed to the Deaf, the Blind, and Individuals with No Sensory Disability," *American Annals of the Deaf* 141 (1996): 24–28.

[14] D. Gottlieb, "Teaching and Students: The Views of Negro and White Teachers," *Sociology of Education* 37 (1964): 345–353.

[15] Robert D. Felner, Stephen Brand, David L. DuBois, Angela M. Adan, Peter F. Mulhall, and Elizabeth G. Evans, "Socioeconomic Disadvantage, Proximal Environmental Experiences, and Socioemotional and Academic Adjustment in Early Adolescence: Investigation of a Mediated Effects Model," *Child Development* 66 (1995): 774–792.

[16] Erikson, *Adulthood.*

[17] Erik H. Erikson, *Identity and the Life Cycle* (New York: W. W. Norton, 1994).

THE ROLE OF ETHICS IN THE UNDERGRADUATE CURRICULUM

Joya Uraizee
Department of English

Introduction

The English Department at Saint Louis University deals with ethics in the sense that we do expect our undergraduate students to be able to pick out and analyze ethical issues as they surface in literary works. For example, we expect our students as well as ourselves, as faculty, who read texts written by writers as diverse as Shakespeare and Alice Walker, to be able to describe the historical and political realities that surround their texts as well as critique the writers' depictions of art and culture. We also encourage our students and our colleagues to respect other people's viewpoints as they appear both in literary texts/theories, and in the classroom, so that they can appreciate what is being said even if they may not agree with it. Moreover, we discourage our students from putting subjective and biased opinions about literature and culture into their papers, and we try to inculcate in them sensitivity to issues of race, class, and gender, as they write. Finally, we hope that our students, and ourselves, will be more open to, and appreciative of, literature in all its diversity after they've taken our courses, simply because they have had to read, reflect, and write about it frequently and critically.

The Integration of Ethics in Literature Courses

Ethics has everything to do with what and how we read and discuss literature and culture in my undergraduate literature courses. First, this is because the multicultural texts that I use deal with issues related to race, class, and gender. Since I teach postcolonial literature and cultural studies, this means I focus on contemporary texts written by writers from Africa, Asia, the Caribbean and Latin America, in English or in English translation. For example, I frequently teach a novel called *Things Fall Apart* written by Nigerian novelist Chinua Achebe.[1] This novel deals with precolonial and colonial Nigeria in the late eighteenth to early nineteenth centuries, and shows how European colonialism destroyed the society that existed then. In introducing the novel to my students, I provide them with maps of Nigeria, several handouts on Nigerian history and culture, as well as a synopsis of Achebe's life. Then, I begin discussing why Achebe chose this topic to write about. I focus on his statement in an interview that his main agenda was to show that, "African people did not hear of culture for the first time from Europeans; that their societies were not mindless but frequently had a philosophy of great depth and value and beauty, that they had poetry, and, above all, they had dignity. It is this dignity that African people all but lost during the colonial period, and it is this that they must now regain."[2] I show how Achebe develops this theme through his plot structure, such that the longest part of the novel is the first part, which describes precolonial Nigerian society in great detail, and also introduces us to the protagonist, Okonkwo, and his family. The shorter parts are parts two and three, which describe the coming of European missionaries and their breaking up of Nigerian communal harmony. I also touch on other themes, such as the novel's call for balance in society, and the destabilizing effect that colonialism had on Africa.

From this example, it should be clear that the voices, ideas, and concepts that I teach belong to, or originate with, individuals and groups that have, through the centuries, been silenced, marginalized, and oppressed. I advocate reading about, and learning from, these groups, who have been disenfranchized and discriminated against. So just the act of recovering them and making them available for my students is, in itself, an ethical or moral act, because it enables some of us to hear those who, historically, have had no voices in dominant discourse or no places in dominant political hierarchies.

Second, the question of justice is very relevant to what I teach because I not only make my students aware that such oppressed but talented writers exist, but I also try to show them how such people are intrinsically worthy of respect, justice, and dignity, and how frequently they are silenced by dominant social and political structures and groups. I show connections between different kinds of oppression, as they appear in literary texts, such that students see that injustices like racism, sexism, and class-based oppression are all connected and are all equally unjust. As Jennifer Daryl Slack and Laurie Anne Whitt suggest:

> The challenge [for cultural critics] becomes to theorize the connections between gender, race, class, etc., that is, to analyze

and critique the ways in which they are articulated.
Recognizing that cultural studies cannot adequately ground its
interventionist strategy by appealing to a *single* principle
(class, gender, or race), cultural theorists [should] ... shift their
concern to the articulating principles that *connect* gender, race,
and class, principles in which relations of subordination and
domination are entailed.[3]

So, in my classroom, we try to discuss how many different sorts of
prejudices and ignorance create misunderstanding and oppression. For
example, I often teach a long epic poem called *I Is a Long Memoried
Woman* by Caribbean poet Grace Nichols.[4] In that poem, the poet-
speaker, a "long-memoried" Afro-Caribbean woman, takes a spiritual
and revolutionary journey back to her past in Africa, and in doing so,
traces the history of her race, transported in slavery from West Africa to
the Caribbean, through the Middle Passage. The poem describes a set of
events in the life of the long memoried woman, including her capture in
Africa, her work as a slave in the sugar cane plantations in the
Caribbean, her sexual abuse by the white slave master, her desire for
revenge, and finally, her acquisition of a new identity which is closely
tied to her body and her power of speech. In discussing this poem, I
provide my students with maps of the middle passage and information
about the slave trade in the sixteenth through nineteenth centuries,
including numbers captured, living conditions on the slave ships, what
the slaves were traded for, etc. I also provide several handouts explaining West African cultural and religious concepts that Nichols uses
frequently in her poem. I draw attention to the fact that the long
memoried woman is oppressed in three ways: due to her race, her class,
and her gender, pointing out that all three serve to silence and oppress
her, and prevent her history from being heard.

Third, I try to suggest that when social structures and institutions in
different cultures across the world learn to treat all groups within those
cultures with dignity, a better society for all will be the result. My aim
in class is not merely to describe or explain contemporary cultural and
literary practices but to initiate changes in thinking about them, and
therefore, bring about changes in society itself. Although this may sound
utopian, there is a sense, in my classes, that we, as students of literature
and culture, can create a better world by educating ourselves about all
the groups within it, especially those that are least like ourselves. In
doing this I like to use a play called "The Trials of Brother Jero" by
Nobel Prize–winning playwright Wole Soyinka, from Nigeria.[5] Since it

is a satire of the hypocrisies of Nigerian religious and political leaders, I use it to talk about corruption and injustice in Nigerian and Western societies, and to figure out the possibilities for change. For example, we analyze how the character, Chume, is spiritually and emotionally dependent on the false prophet, Brother Jeroboam, and how Soyinka uses him to suggest that dependency is the key to power. We examine the fact that in plays like this, Nigerian leaders appear to be quite corrupt, and seem to perpetuate an unjust society. We try to figure out ways in which their ability to control the lives of others could be reduced.

Pedagogical Methods

In presenting the literature and culture that I teach, I also try to make certain choices that have to do with moral or justice concerns.

First, I try to ensure that all the students in my classes do get a chance to voice their opinions, participate in discussions, and make their own decisions about culture on their own terms. I act as moderator, not controller, and hope that in so doing, I don't fall prey to subordinating my students to the very same power structures that they read about as being oppressive and hierarchical. For example, I use small group techniques when I teach the novel *Cracking India* by Pakistani novelist Bapsi Sidhwa.[6] After providing my students with historical and cultural data about India and Pakistan, I give them several homework assignments which they do individually and then discuss in groups in class, before presenting their responses to me. Some assignments include explaining how India was partitioned or divided up in 1947; others involve finding out what the main beliefs and practices of the Zoroastrians are, since they are the religious group that is at the focus in the novel. I then devise several in-class assignments for them, such as questions about the protagonist, Lenny's, relationships with her family and her community; the kinds of roles that the antagonist, Ice Candy Man, plays; the sorts of relationships that Sikh and Muslim villagers have with each other before the Partition; examples of religious bigotry after the Partition, and so on. I type up these questions and make them into several handouts, which the students then work their way through in small groups of two or three. I then ask the students to present their ideas to the class, and we compare how each group's answers relate to each other. I find that frequently, students who feel uncomfortable voicing their opinions on matters of race or religion or gender in class, are somewhat less inhibited in small groups; thus, class participation is good and everyone's opinion counts.

Second, I recognize that the students are participating in cultural practices even when they are discussing and disagreeing with literary and cultural texts in the classroom, and I see that as inherently creative. For example, students are often very divided in their responses to some poems by minority American poets, such as to African-American poet Nikki Giovanni's "Nikki-Rosa."[7] In discussing the speaker's statement that she'd rather not have white biographers write histories of her life because they'd never understand its richness, fairly heated arguments frequently break out in class. Although student opinions seem divided on racial lines, frequently the disagreements do lead to some grudging acknowledgment of some amount of truth or validity in the other side's position. And thus, we all learn from each other.

Conclusion

I am concerned not necessarily about my students' knowledge of the theories of philosophers and theologians, although, of course, that is very important, but more about the existence of such evils as ethnocentrism and racial, sexual, or class-based stereotyping on campus. Quite often, I find that when reading about or discussing works of literature from other cultures, or even from minority cultures within the United States, students can be surprised by the fact that, as Mary Louise Pratt puts it, "people and groups are constituted not by single unified belief systems, but by competing, self-contradictory ones."[8] I worry that either I as instructor, or my students, might regard other cultural practices as uniform and fixed, and remain blind to ethnic, racial, sexual, class-based, and generational differences within those practices. I fear that some of us may stereotype people from other cultures as static or one-sided, allowing ourselves to be influenced by what we may have heard or seen in commercial cinema or media. At the same time, I would be happy if, when we compare our own culture to a different one, we see our own experiences as being multicultural, or, as moving between and within different communities in our own culture.[9] I hope that in my classes, students get an opportunity to move across various sorts of borders, and thereby understand and appreciate their own cultures as well as other ones. Above all, I hope that they may promote individual and communal subjectivities and be more aware of their own roles in shaping cultural practices.

Notes

[1] Chinua Achebe, *Things Fall Apart* (New York: Anchor/Doubleday, 1994).

[2] Chinua Achebe, "The Role of the Writer in the New Nation," *Nigeria Magazine* (June 1964): n.p.

[3] Jennifer Daryl Slack and Laurie Anne Whitt, "Ethics and Cultural Studies," in *Cultural Studies*, ed. Lawrence Grossberg, Cary Nelson, and Paula A. Treichler (New York: Routledge, 1992), 571–592.

[4] Grace Nichols, *I Is a Long Memoried Woman* (London: Karnak, 1983; reprint, Lawrenceville: Red Sea Press, 1990).

[5] Wole Soyinka, *The Trials of Brother Jero and the Strong Breed* (New York: Dramatists Play Service, 1992).

[6] Bapsi Sidhwa, *Cracking India* (Minneapolis: Milkweed, 1991).

[7] Nikki Giovanni, "Nikki-Rosa," in *Trouble the Water: 250 Years of African American Poetry*, ed. Jerry W. Ward, Jr. (New York: Mentor, 1997), 419.

[8] Mary Louis Pratt, "Interpretative Strategies/Strategic Interpretations: On Anglo-American Reader Response Criticism," *Boundary* 211, no. 1–2 (fall/winter 1982–83): 228.

[9] Delores K. Schriner, "One Person, Many Worlds: A Multi-cultural Composition Curriculum," in *Cultural Studies in the English Classroom*, ed. James A. Berlin and Michael J. Vivion (Portsmouth: Boynton/Cook Heinemann, 1992), 98.

ETHICAL ISSUES IN UNDERGRADUATE EDUCATION: A BIOLOGIST'S VIEW

Robert Bolla
Department of Biology

Faculty teaching the biological sciences in this day and age have as many ethical issues to present to undergraduate students as the undergraduate students have to think about as they process through their education to graduation. Our students are going to become doctors, dentists, or other medical professionals, veterinarians, teachers, academics, or researchers. Many of the students will enter research careers in pharmaceutical companies, in the food industry, or in the environmental management and regulation industry. They will also enter federal research laboratories and perhaps the political arena. When we realize this, we realize that our graduates will have a future effect on many aspects of our lives. As academics, we have the responsibility to provide our students with a framework from which they can make the ethical decisions that arise daily in their professions as scientists. In biology we strive to raise the questions and encourage the students to think about them. We rely on the philosophers and theologians to build the platform that helps the students make their decisions.

Using this paper as a vehicle, I would like to make you aware of the environment in which we teach biology today and the questions we must consider. I will ask many questions, but I will provide few answers. My task is to help you begin to image the difficulty our graduates will face as they enter their professions.

The last two decades have been a revolution for the biological, agricultural, and biomedical sciences. This revolution has come about through development of the technology of genetic engineering and the pressures placed on the environment by the need to expand the world food supply. Driven by the quest to better understand genetics, biologists have developed the technology needed to isolate, clone, and sequence genomes from a variety of organisms. We have sequenced the genomes of representative bacteria and yeast and of a multicellular worm *Caenorhabditis elegans*, and the weedy plant *Arabdopsis thalania*. The sequence of one or more additional plant genomes will be completed within the year. Within the next five years, we should have the sequence of the genomes of major crop plants. We are only three to five years away from completing the sequence of the "model" human genome. Our efforts have not stopped here as we have developed technology needed for cloning animals from nonreproductive tissue and for genetically engineering plants for protection against pathogens and abiotic stresses and for increased crop yield. Although the technology is not yet refined, we can genetically engineer some animals with some degree of efficiency. This revolution shows no signs of stopping or slowing and daily we are confronted with a new discovery. As the past two centuries have been labeled "Centuries of Physics and Chemistry," the next century has been called by some the "Century of Biology."

This quest to better understand genetic control of the function of organisms also has led to the development of physical maps of several plant and animal genomes. These maps let us locate specific functional genes and capture these genes for our benefit. We have isolated new genes with potential commercial benefit from plants and animals and we have genetically engineered bacteria and yeast as factories for commercial production of everything from growth hormone to dye for blue jeans. We have cloned sheep and mice from nonreproductive cells showing that we can clone organisms outside of reproductive function. We have transplanted neurogenic stem cells into the brains of mice to improve neurological conditions and we are developing a similar approach to treating Parkinson's disease in humans with transplanted human neurogenic stem cells. We have tested genetic engineering of children to "cure" severe immunodeficiency syndrome (SCID, bubble baby syndrome). We have identified the sequences of genes involved in several inherited diseases of metabolism and have discovered genes associated with several types of cancer. We now have the ability to diagnose diseases such as familial Alzheimer's disease, Huntington's disease, and cystic fibrosis, among others. We are now able to identify those individuals at risk for such cancers as breast cancer. Other biochemical technology of this decade has provided prenatal testing for a wide variety of genetic diseases.

Our successes are not only with humans or animals, but are also seen in agricultural production. Using bovine growth hormone produced in genetically altered bacteria, we can increase milk production in cattle or, using bacterial synthesized porcine hormone, we can produce leaner pork. We have genetically engineered plants for herbicide and insect resistance. Thus, we have used the new technology to improve farming methods while removing some chemical pesticides from the environment. We have genetically engineered tomato for controlled ripening so that those that reach your table taste "vine-ripe" even during the winter. We use genetically engineered bacteria to prevent strawberries from freezing so that this fresh fruit is on the market longer each year. We are producing human proteins in plants. A single field of tobacco can produce enough human insulin to fill a single year's demand. This list could go on and on.

The new genetic technology is not, however, the only technology bringing new discoveries for improving the human condition or for safely feeding the growing world population. Many older technologies are melding with the new technology to move the biosciences rapidly forward. These developments are bounded only by what we set as goals within an ethical framework of use. Each new breakthrough seems to introduce new ethical issues and problems. For example, should we proceed with experiments on cloning animals knowing that this technology could be applied to cloning of humans? Is it ethical to patent genes or proteins? If we can identify genetic mutations from gene sequence, should we do prenatal diagnosis by choice or by routine? What if a prenatal diagnosis identifies a debilitating disease? Now, for example, all babies are tested for phenylketonuria (PKU) since this genetic condition can be managed and healthy lives develop. How far should we extend mandatory disease diagnosis? Who should know the results: the individual, the insurance company, or the employer? Should we develop an artificial blood for transfusion? Is it all right to put a gene for herbicide resistance or other genes in a food crop plant without knowing all of the potential side effects or the risk to the environment? Where should chemical improvement of crop production end and genetic improvement begin? In the end, perhaps the biggest questions are these: How do we decide who benefits from the development of biological discoveries and how do we assure a fair distribution of the discoveries for the common good?

The biological revolution was initially driven by our desire to learn more about how genetics controls the function of organisms. As discoveries were made, however, the driving forces became more practical and "commercial." With the greater availability of technology and continued technological advances, we are more and more driven by our desire to avoid the specter of disease and death, by a desire for social control, and by a need to control the environment for our needs. Thus, we began to look for ways to diagnose and treat diseases, to predict the emergence of new diseases, and to determine individuals at risk for genetically inherited diseases and cancer. We began trying to implicate genetic background in social behaviors such as tendency toward violence or alcoholism. We began to devise ways to use the new biotechnology to more effectively produce food crops and increase crop and livestock yield to feed a growing world population. There is an increasing monetary aspect to the rapid movement forward of bioscience. Our biggest drive for new knowledge is our belief that as individuals we ought to have the freedom to search for and use new knowledge for our gains.

There is considerable good that can come from biology as it continues to better understand the function of living organisms if we realize that with each step forward a new ethical dilemma is created. This is where our responsibilities as academics enter the picture. We must realize that we have to discuss the issues of the new technology with our students.

In looking at the teaching of ethics in undergraduate education, I would like to consider the ethical issues biologists must face today and in the not so distant future as we teach, do research, and prepare students for their role as scientists. That is, I would like to discuss what our students will have to think about.

Before going any further, I would like to put the discussion into a limiting framework. Biologists are very pragmatic and we put limits on what we can and cannot do in discovering new knowledge. If we ask a question, we must be able to put the question into a testable hypothesis, design experiments to refute or support the hypothesis, and talk about the hypothesis in a historical context. That is, we must discuss our findings in relation to the findings of others and we must realize that our hypothesis is always testable by others. We can draw no conclusions about the past, present, or future without testing a hypothesis nor can we prove anything concretely right or wrong. We each have an ethical approach to what we do and how we do it, and we each have an opinion about what our findings mean for the future. Our approach and our opinions are based on life-long learning, on our experience within society, and on what we hypothesize and learn in the lab. We must perpetuate this framework of science for undergraduates.

With this as an escape from a scientist's propensity to state everything in his or her realm as founded fact, I would like to approach the issue of providing a framework of ethical thought to undergraduates studying the biological sciences. I will address the ethical issues we now face in the classroom, the lab, and what I will call "the neighborhood." I will raise many questions but I will provide no answers.

In the Classroom

Let's begin in the classroom. As freshmen settle into their first laboratory sessions, they are told to work independently, but that they will work in teams of three or four to make observations and collect data. Laboratory reports, on the other hand, will be independent pieces of work. Now we have a quandary: How can we work together and write an independent report? The instructor tells the students that copying or sharing laboratory reports is plagiarism and that there is a stiff penalty for this foul, unethical occurrence. As the pressures build in the semester, students begin asking why they cannot each submit the same report. The students begin to raise several questions. What's wrong if we just change a few words so that the report looks different? Why can't I have my roommate who is in another lab section write the report for me or why don't I just borrow my roommate's report? Wasn't this lab done last year and, if so, why don't I just look for an old report, change a few words, and submit it as my own? Why can't we just write one report for the group?

Realizing that these questions arise, we are very careful in our laboratory teaching to explain our goals and to make the students understand that we are teaching them to use their observational skills to draw conclusions or to learn facts. We want them to understand that these skills are enhanced by collaboration with colleagues, and that sharing of ideas can lead to discoveries but that independence in thought and interpretation is required to fully understand discovery. We want them to realize that when they enter the "real world" much of what they do will be a team effort. Often a single team-generated report will describe the conclusions of their work, but each member of the team will be held responsible for the content. These explanations aside, are our expectations really ethical in themselves? Should we not ask for team reports each written by a different member of the team each time and hold each member of the team responsible for the work? That is, should we create reality in the artificial world of education and remove the ethical challenge we present the students, or is what we expect just another learning experience about ethical decision making?

If, for a moment, we leave the teaching laboratory and go to the classroom, there are other ethical considerations we must discuss. How do we define cheating? When it comes to examinations this is easily done, but what about writing papers? We encourage writing in our courses as it is key to our profession. This often means a visit to, and analysis of, the literature to answer a specific question or to put our work in contest of others' findings. We must teach our students to read and interpret literature. The biggest problem is to make students understand that writing must be original. Paraphrasing by just changing a few words is as much plagiarism as is directly stealing the passage without quoting or giving credit. We spend a significant amount of time introducing the concept of how to cite literature and what can be done in putting others' ideas into your writing. Today, we are faced with yet another challenge, i.e., the World Wide Web. There are no guidelines for citing Web sources in the sciences and it is difficult to identify "stolen" material; in fact, entire papers can be captured from the Web. How do we provide an environment for students to understand the ethics of doing their own work when many are under the pressure of many assignments or the pressure to maintain a high grade-point average?

In summary, there are many academic issues that arise as we educate our students. These issues and their importance are influenced by the discipline and by the educational environment. The issues of the laboratory are not necessarily the issues of the classroom, although one may influence the other. It is important that students hear about these issues, and that we provide them with the tools to think about them. As scientists, however, the answers to the many ethical questions or the approach to be taken to reach an ethical conclusion lie outside the focus of our disciplines, and for the most part, our training. We leave this to the classrooms in philosophy and theological studies.

In Research

Our undergraduates are encouraged to do independent research in a faculty laboratory. This opens a Pandora's box of ethical issues. If a student is working in a laboratory with a project using animals, we must provide the student with the principles of ethical use of animals in research. The student must understand how to treat the animals so that any procedure is met with the minimal level of discomfort and the maximum level of safety. The student must learn how to decide whether the animal actually must be used for the experiment or whether a model system would work as well. We must have the student researchers feel comfortable enough to question the faculty member, graduate student, or postdoctoral researcher if there ever is an uneasiness of how the animal is being treated or if the experiment wanders from the procedures approved by the animal use committee. If the laboratory is involved in research using human subjects, we must provide a background to the ethical issues involved. This is unusual for undergraduate research projects in biology, but is a consideration.

Perhaps the most important issue in research is that of "fudging" data. In other words, we have to provide our undergraduates with the culture of how experiments are done and how data are collected. They have to learn to record what they see, not what they feel that they should see, regardless of the pressures they are under to complete a project. It is hard to teach that failure is the usual in experimental sciences and that failure is okay. The students must learn that the experimental design is important and that controls known to give positive as well as negative results must be included whenever possible.

A second issue is to teach that it is okay to exactly repeat someone's research, that this is not plagiarism. Science often is based on reevaluating someone's hypothesis, or using someone's approach to test the hypothesis in another model system. But we cannot simply report another's data as our own. Often the best teacher is example. I have three true stories that address issues of ethical research practices to share with my students. There is the story of the scientist who obtained obscure foreign journals, lifted the data directly, claimed the data as his own, and then wrote a "research" article for an American journal. He was caught when a Japanese scientist picked up a manuscript in preparation. The second story is that of a scientist under pressure from his funding agency and employer to provide a conclusion to a controversial study. This scientist fabricated his data by changing a few of the observational numbers. He is no longer employed and his postdoctoral student, who had nothing to do with the misrepresentation of data, nearly had his career ruined. The final story is that of David Baltimore, winner of a Nobel Prize in Medicine. A postdoctoral fellow in Dr. Baltimore's laboratory chose to alter the observational data and to embellish a manuscript. This was discovered and investigated by the NIH. Because Baltimore's name was on the paper, both he and the postdoctoral fellow were held responsible for a breach of research ethics.

Is it ever ethical to use someone else's data to test your own hypothesis or, in fact, use these data in a form different from that in which they were published? The answer is yes. We do it routinely as we write review papers. But we ask permission and cite sources. For example, we accumulate large volumes of data from the various genome projects into public domain databases. The data are then available to all and can be analyzed in many ways to obtain different answers to a variety of questions. We just have to cite the source of the information. Published and Web-based data are the realm of scientists whose research is in modeling. It becomes difficult to teach students that it is okay to develop a hypothesis which requires the use of another's data for testing, but it is not okay to directly copy another's tables or graphs into a report that you claim as your own.

An important issue now on the table is the question of ownership of data. If you are an undergraduate student working on an independent research project in a faculty member's laboratory, as part of a larger project funded by NIH or NSF for example, who owns the data you have collected? This is a very important discussion today for several reasons. Faculty and students are mobile and careers often are based on research efforts. Students want papers to ease their way into the best graduate or professional schools or to round out their résumé in job hunting; the faculty member wants the research data to apply for his/her next grant. Maybe the data are so unique that they might lead to a patent and possibility of an economic profit for the lab and the university. Perhaps the student wants to continue the research in graduate school. Just who owns the data? Ethically, can the faculty member claim the data because he/she assigned the project, designed the experiments, and provided funding? Can the university or the funding agency demand the data? A recent bill passed in Congress says that data collected through a publicly funded project belongs to the public and all notebooks have to be open to all. What does this mean? Can a company come in and use your ideas for their profit? Can this company develop your data to a patent or use the data for a major commercial venture without compensating you? This alone creates all sorts of ethical issues for the faculty and the university and is something about which students must be aware.

A second issue of data ownership comes when it is time to publish. Whose name goes first on the paper, i.e., who gets top billing? Is it necessary that a faculty member include the name of a student on a paper if the student contributed just a small piece of the information that led to the conclusions drawn or is an acknowledgment enough? In fact, if the student's contribution is only a small part of the overall project, is it ethical to assign that student an authorship? What if the student completes an assigned project and alone collects enough data for publication? The idea came from the faculty member, the faculty member probably designed the experiment and taught the student the technology needed for the work, but the student did all of the bench work and perhaps modified the method for better applicability. That is, the student had real intellectual input. In the end, the faculty member writes the paper. Now who should be able to claim the first or major authorship?

As there is increased funding of research through contracts with private companies, commodity groups, or private foundations, and a lesser role of public funding, a third issue of ownership enters the research arena. With the new biology developments around gene discovery, informatics, and method development, more and more universities are supporting research through the development or licensing of intellectual property or by supporting faculty in the development of spin-off companies. The thought of developing new businesses based on their ideas is driving more and more faculty to think of a payoff from their research. If students work in a laboratory, what is their role in development and ownership of intellectual property? There are clear legal definitions to cover some relationships, but others remain clouded. For example, if a student works in the lab for pay and is assigned a specific task for which no intellectual input is expected, this is "work for hire" and the data and intellectual property clearly belong to the principal investigator. The issues become clouded once the student truly begins to contribute to discovery. Although there may not be a clear answer to some relationships in research, we must make our students aware of their roles and their proprietary relationships to the research. We must teach our students the ethics of discussing the research freely when this may be limited by agreements between the lab and the funding source. Students have to learn the difference between public and private domain with regard to usage of research results.

Depending on the focus of the laboratory, there are many other ethical questions that arise. Is it ethical to put an experimental chemical into the environment to collect data for an experiment you have designed? If you are working on an endangered species and you need a DNA sample, is it okay to kill just one of the species? What are the limits of your discovery? In other words, how global is your discovery? Does it apply to just a certain situation or does it apply to the entire biological world? You must make this decision if you publish or talk about your data. Is it ethical to patent a gene and remove the gene sequence from the public domain? How about a protein, bacteria, a modified plant, or other organism?

To summarize, most research scientists are well aware of the ethical issues affecting how they do their work, as most issues are specific to a scientific subdiscipline. Most scientists are well versed in the ethical approach to research, to the use of animals and humans in research, and to the use of other methods and data. They gain their ethics from the culture in which they are raised and work. Most scientists can give you a reasoned opinion on ethical issues of patenting biological materials, on manipulation of the environment for research purposes, or on working with genetic information. It is important that we pass this culture on by teaching undergraduate students ethical approaches to science.

In the Neighborhood

Finally, let's turn our attention to the ethical issues students majoring in the life sciences will face as they enter upon a career or continue their education. Biology today is challenged on several fronts and our students need to be aware of the issues of modern bioscience. They must be able to think about them and they should have a foundation from which to support an ethical decision. Rather than address the many growing issues directly, I will leave you with a series of questions we raise for our students in our curriculum in biology.

Within the next decade we will have a sequence map of the human genome and from this we will know the position and function of many genes. During this same decade we will be challenged to find better ways to feed the world and will have to address how this influences the environment. More and more species of animals and plants will become endangered as we expand our living and working space and as agriculture expands to meet world demands for food. As the baby-boomer generation ages, there will be more and more emphasis put on extending the life span or at least in extending the healthy part of the life span. As new technologies are developed, more and more people are affected either directly or indirectly by them and how we look at life changes drastically.

It will be necessary to develop better technology of food production to feed a rapidly growing world population. Thus, there is a major emphasis on crop improvement and production using genetic engineering. Major seed producers are developing easier ways of farming, better ways to protect crops against pathogens, or ways to increase yield. Designer corn, wheat, and soybean are not far off. Livestock producers are focusing on new technologies to provide a larger, leaner meat production, or to increase milk and poultry production.

A major issue is whether or not we can release genetically engineered organisms into the environment without fully understanding the biology of the organism and its effect on the stability of the ecosystem. If we release an herbicide-resistant plant into the environment, is it important that we know whether the gene for herbicide resistance can jump into other plants including weeds. Do we need to know the effect of this gene on the food chain? If we produce bovine growth hormone in bacteria to inject and enhance milk or meat production, must we consider the effects of this technology on human health? How do we insure that a harmful gene product doesn't get into the food chain? What control should the public have on the private sector that is developing the technology for profit? Is gene development a free market or should there be controls?

Many labs isolate and clone new or different genes almost daily. What are the ethical issues of patenting genes? Should we maintain genes for private use or should they become public domain? If genes can be used to better the human condition, how should they be used? Who should benefit from genetic engineering? Where do we separate private ends from the common good?

We can clone animals from somatic cells. What are the issues associated with cloning of humans? Is this something we should think of doing? What about cloning animals for agricultural use? We already clone plants through selective breeding programs using old technology and in this way improve crop yield.

Medical science has perfected organ transplant, but there is a limited number of donor organs available. This raises all sorts of questions. Let's look at one example. Our genome is about 98% similar to that of chimpanzees. Apes have 24 pairs of chromosomes while humans have 23 pairs. Eighteen of 23 pairs are virtually identical in humans and other apes. Segments of the remaining pairs have been reshuffled in evolution. A good demonstration of this is the gene of the movie *Lorenzo's Oil*. This gene is involved in the genetically inherited disease adrenoleukodystrophy. It is on the X chromosome in chimps and humans, but nonfunctional copies are found scattered throughout the chimp genome. Genes clearly are reshuffled on chromosomes 4, 6, 9, and 12 when humans and chimps are compared. Some of the differences are involved in expression of tissue specificity. What if we knew the regions of the chromosomes that differ and were able to replace the simian genes with their human counterpart from specific individuals? If we did this, the organs of the simian should carry the tissue type of an individual human. Could we now use apes for tissue farming? This would be expensive. Would it then be available to only the wealthy? Is this something we should think of developing? What might the consequences be? Are we far off in the discovery of this technology? In my opinion, probably not.

Next, let me address issues of genetic modification for treatment of genetic diseases, genetic diagnostics of human diseases, and the issue of using genetically engineered organisms in weapons development.

As the human genome has evolved, we have identified genes associated with several human diseases. These include, among others, human familial breast cancer, familial Alzheimer's disease, Lou Gehrig's disease, retinal blastoma, Huntington's disease, cystic fibrosis, SCID (severe immunodeficiency syndrome, bubble baby syndrome), Down's syndrome, and the fragile X syndrome. With these genes in hand we are ready to apply some of the new technology. But let's think a minute. How far do we want to go with this technology and what problems might arise? If you knew there was Alzheimer's disease in your family would you, or should you, know whether you were a carrier of a gene that would indicate that you are at risk? What if this gene was found and the information became available to your insurance company? Suppose there was a history of breast cancer in your family. How young should you be to undergo a genetic diagnosis to see if you were a carrier of the gene that would indicate, but not insure, that you were at risk? Again, should your insurance company know? Do you have your daughter diagnosed? If so, when? Do we demand genetic diagnosis for those genes we have available so that we can plan ahead for medical care? Should employers or insurance companies be able to demand the results of genetic diagnosis? What effect might this have on employment or insurability?

A second rapidly developing area is the genetic engineering of human cells. This introduces a plethora of questions. What about genetically engineering stem cells to replace a bad gene or bad gene product with a good gene or good gene product? Is this something we should make an effort to perfect in the lab? Should we genetically engineer reproductive cells so that the engineered product is vertically inherited and thus once the gene is in a germ line it is always there? Should we limit our gene manipulation to somatic tissue to prevent inheritance into subsequent generations? Should we be able to work to genetically modify stem cells and use these to replace gene function as a routine method of therapy? To date there has been some success in engineering hemopoetic stem cells with the gene missing in SCID, and transplanting these cells into an affected child. With the aid of chemotherapy, the child is now able to lead a fairly normal life. Taken along with artificial reproductive technology, how far should we go in genetic engineering of humans? Will we reach a point when parents will want to design children with specific eye or hair color and other characters? What should we do about this? How far might this technology go and what controls should be placed on it? What about embryo manipulation to improve the genetic condition?

Finally, let's look at the issue of biological warfare. We can now genetically engineer some scary organisms. There is ongoing debate about the destruction of our remaining supplies of small pox held at the CDC. The only other known small pox in the world is in Moscow. Should we keep our supply in case someone decides to use this virus to design a biological weapon? Remember this disease has been defined as eradicated and we no longer vaccinate for it. That means the population immunity is greatly reduced. Recently a protein signal sequence from the AIDS virus has been identified that, when genetically engineered onto any protein, induces this protein to cross a membrane within a few seconds or minutes of exposure. What if we genetically engineered a bacterium to produce a toxin with this signal protein attached?

In summary, the new biology raises many ethical issues about the environment and about what we do with our genetic knowledge. These issues will have to be addressed by the present generation of students as they assume careers or become effective citizens involved in policy-making. We, as educators and biologists, have the responsibility to raise the questions. We have the responsibility to provide our students with the scientific background to intelligently discuss the issues and begin to make decisions about them. To fulfill our role, faculty members in the Biology Department raise these issues in as many classes as possible and provide a forum for the students to think about, write about, and talk about them. We depend, however, on background foundations from philosophy and theology to give the platform from which the students build their ethical thoughts and make reasoned ethical decisions. That is, we depend on these disciplines to help students learn how to think about and make the right decisions, not just decisions that fulfill their own goals but decisions that affect the greater common good.

ETHICS ACROSS THE CURRICULUM: IT IS WORKING

Avis E. Meyer
Department of Communication

Good afternoon. As I mentioned to Professor Tuchler this morning, I intend to follow three rules of speaking bequeathed to me by one of my mentors: Be organized, be entertaining, be seated.

The ethical foundations that arise in my journalism classes include several whose names have been mentioned by colleagues who have spoken here today. The list includes Milton, Descartes, Bacon, Hobbes, Mill, Jefferson, James, Lippmann . . . and on, and on.

As Mark Chmiel mentioned, I too, try to nurture an ethical code. And as Jim Fisher noted, I use examples and anecdotes to illustrate ethical behavior and standards. I share with my students those people in my life who have become my personal touchstones: my grandmother, my wife, Fr. John Kavanaugh, and Fr. Maurice MacNamee, to name but a few.

I believe that compassion is an inextricable facet of ethics. For how can one behave ethically unless a concern for your fellow human beings is at the core?

I think that the best way to conclude this symposium is to share a few experiences that should serve to remind us that our efforts are not in vain. Our students do respond to pressure with grace, to challenges with ethical behavior, and to others with compassion.

Five years ago. I attended the funeral of a young man's mother. He was 22 and struggling to maintain control, even as he stood before the crowd at the memorial service to speak about his mother. He recalled a solo that he had to sing in fourth grade. He remembered that he was so nervous, that his mouth was dry, that the lump in his throat was rising. As he stood with other members of the chorus, the moment of his solo drawing nearer, his eyes met his mother's eyes. She looked at him with a firm smile, and slowly, silently mouthed two words, twice: "Go on. Go on." Then he said that he thought she would tell us the very same thing, now. Go on.

His uncle spoke next. As he was remembering his sister and the long life they had shared, Tim was standing slightly behind his uncle's right shoulder. When his uncle faltered and fell silent with grief, Tim discarded his grief, took a step forward, and placed his left hand in the middle of his uncle's back and said, almost imperceptibly, "Go on." And his uncle did.

About ten years ago, one of my best students—now a big shot in P.R. at Anheuser-Busch—sent an anonymous poem to the editors of what was then St. Louis U's oldest and only poetry and prose magazine. As my two co-editors and I read through the submissions, we agreed that the three-stanza poem about the influence of a grandmother on a young grandson was a "keeper." When we had our annual reading at Cupples House, I was surprised to see Charles in the audience. I was even more surprised when he came forward to read the "anonymous" poem.

After the reading, he told me the reason he had maintained his anonymity was because he knew that I held him in high regard, and he wanted his poetry to be chosen on its merits, not his.

Fifteen years ago, a young woman who is now a Ph.D. in English, came to me near the end of her senior year. She was the first to finish a midterm exam on a 200-page text that covered the philosophical development of the American press system. She asked if she might speak to me briefly, in the hallway. There, Kathy asked me if I remembered an advanced class I had allowed her to audit during her freshman year. I told her I did, but wasn't sure what the point was. Well, the point was, she added with a smile, that the test she had just taken was markedly similar to the one that that class had taken and which she had seen four and a half years ago. She added that she felt "sort of awkward" about using that experience to her benefit, when everyone else had had to read the book. We worked it out, of course; and she received an A anyway.

Twenty years ago, a student who always wanted to be a broadcaster stopped by my office just before Thanksgiving break to talk about a big job offer. She had graduated a few years earlier and was working at a radio station in Belleville. She was engaged to a young man who also worked at the station; they were scheduled to be married in early January. I told her that even a small radio station in Buffalo, New York, with a network affiliation seemed to be a step in the right direction, even though it was a big step. She laughed and told me that she had already made the decision; she was just curious if I agreed with her. She was obviously on her way.

Two days after Christmas, I received a phone call from her father. We had met years ago, when Nancy was a freshman, and I remember him at her graduation, beaming with pride at her magna cum laude. He could barely speak. And after he told me about the drunken driver who had hit and killed both Nancy and her fiancé on a rural Illinois road, I could barely listen. "Tell the U-News kids," he said.

I called her best friend, who is now a judge in Clayton; as I struggled to say it, she struggled to understand. I called a few more people; they each said they'd call others. The entire staff was at the funeral.

A month and a half later, as the staff of the newspaper was putting together the Valentine's issue, we got to reminiscing. We decided to write a sort of memorial Valentine for Nancy. We printed it as a guest commentary. It wasn't too long. I still remember the last line: "Twenty-five forever."

When the paper came out Friday afternoon, as it did back then, I swung by Busch Center to pick up a handful of copies with the idea of taking them to Nancy's father. I debated with myself whether or not this would be a balm for his grief or a reminder of it. By six or so in the evening, I found myself near Carondelet Park knocking on her father's front door. When he answered, the stoicism I expected to find on his face was there, but so was a hint of peace. When I explained why I had come, and hesitantly handed him the newspapers, he stepped aside and motioned down the hallway behind him.

There on the small table at the bottom of the stairwell was a stack of seven or eight bunches of school papers—hand delivered by other members of the staff, none of whom had discussed it with anyone else, and all of whom wanted to help somehow.

William James said (and I am paraphrasing) that the discussion of ethics will not be complete until every person has had a chance to discuss every experience with every other person.

So . . . what we are trying to do, it seems to me, is worthwhile and is working. I hope we continue.

Thank you for your kind attention.

ALUMNI AND FACULTY PERCEPTIONS OF VALUES AND ETHICS IN GRADUATE EDUCATION AT SAINT LOUIS UNIVERSITY

Donald G. Brennan
Dean of the Graduate School/
University Research Administrator

and

Ronald E. Modras
Professor of Theological Studies

Introduction

The fact that numerous once-Protestant colleges and universities gradually became thoroughly secular has been offered as a warning to those entrusted with the future of Catholic higher education. There are those who fear that American Catholic colleges and universities may repeat that history with their increasingly successful efforts at becoming respected centers of research, teaching, and community service. Very much aware of that history, concerned Catholic educators have expressed determination to preserve the identity and distinctiveness of their institutions. This certainly is the case at Saint Louis University.

Saint Louis University declares itself in its mission statement to be both Catholic and Jesuit. It professes a Catholic identity even though it is thoroughly committed to academic freedom and is administered under the supervision of a board of trustees who is independent of any outside ecclesiastical control. The university professes a Jesuit identity, even though the vast majority of faculty and administration are not members of the Society of Jesus.

The university justifies its identity as Catholic and Jesuit by affirming, in its mission statement, that its pursuit of knowledge and service are "motivated by the inspiration and values of the Judeo-

Christian tradition" and "guided by the spiritual and intellectual ideals of the Society of Jesus." Those ideals can be summed up as a "spiritual humanism" rooted in the Renaissance origins of the Society of Jesus. They include a commitment to academic excellence, but also to values. Among those values are: educating students to be "men and women for others"; being concerned about the whole person, including the spiritual dimension that lies at the basis of human dignity; affirming and celebrating the diversity of cultures in our world and campus communities; and educating students to become leaders in striving for a more just and humane society.

While these goals and ideals of Jesuit education are distinctive, Saint Louis University—like its sister Jesuit colleges and universities —finds itself in a situation that requires considerable effort to preserve its distinctive identity. It must struggle to balance and compete with a considerable number of external factors. The number of Jesuit professors on campus has declined dramatically, creating a tension in faculty hiring. How does the university maintain a commitment to Jesuit identity and to academic excellence in hiring a predominantly lay professorate? How does it maintain this distinctive identity and also seek religious, ethnic, and racial diversity among our faculty and students? In this changing environment, how does it maintain Jesuit identity and preserve academic freedom? How does the university promote itself to the public in respect to cost, academic quality, and distinctiveness from other institutions of higher education? Is Saint Louis University indeed "different" and what makes it "different"?

Undergraduate students and their parents may be attracted to Jesuit universities because of the reputation of these universities for academic excellence, as well as their commitment to education in the Judeo-Christian tradition. Undergraduate students are required to enroll in a "core curriculum" that includes courses in philosophy and theological studies, and the appreciation of other cultures. The core curriculum exposes these students to the importance of "service to others." Undergraduates also have the opportunity to participate in service organizations, and many experience positive interaction with campus ministers.

What attracts graduate and professional students to our institutions? Is it our Catholic identity, our Jesuit intellectual heritage, or other more "secular and common" reasons varying from the opportunity to study with an outstanding faculty mentor to "my husband works in St. Louis and . . ." Graduate students are highly career-centered and focused on their coursework, their research, their clinical practica, and their laboratories. They are older and have different motivations and objectives than undergraduates. Further, they generally do not share the same university experiences as our undergraduates do. At Saint Louis University, the percentage of Roman Catholic graduate students is considerably lower than the percentage of Roman Catholic undergraduates. Are graduate and professional students more interested in the academic reputation of their program rather than its Jesuit, Catholic identity? If so, is our Jesuit, Catholic graduate education distinctive from secular universities?

In 1993, the Graduate School developed a mandatory "Exit Questionnaire" for all graduating graduate students. The questionnaire provided both quantitative and qualitative data in that students rated each item on a Likert-type index ("5" strongly agree to "1" strongly disagree) and then commented on the question. The sixth item on this questionnaire stated: "My graduate education at Saint Louis University reflected an ethical and value dimension consistent with the university's mission." In a three-year period, 1993–1996, 1,189 graduate students responded to the questionnaire. The mean score for all respondents to the sixth item was 4.26; the median was 4.00; and, the mode was 5.00 (Table 1). Clearly these data support a hypothesis that graduate students at Saint Louis University perceived that their graduate education reflected a values/ethics dimension consistent with the university's mission.

TABLE 1: Mean, Median and Mode Scores of Graduate Students on Question Six of the Exit Questionnaire

"MY GRADUATE EDUCATION AT SAINT LOUIS UNIVERSITY
REFLECTED AN ETHICAL AND VALUE DIMENSION
CONSISTENT WITH THE UNIVERSITY'S MISSION."

	1993–94	1994–95	1995–96	Total
NUMBER OF RESPONDENTS	427	370	392	1,189
MEAN SCORE	4.25	4.22	4.31	4.26
MEDIAN SCORE	4.00	4.00	5.00	4.00
MODE	5.00	5.00	5.00	5.00

The unique dimensions of a Jesuit education are frequently substantiated by anecdotal and personal experiences. The descriptive statistics cited above provide more than anecdotal support, but student comments to this question clearly suggested the need for further study.

The purpose of this current research was to investigate the underlying components of the graduate students' positive ratings of the ethical and value dimension experienced during their graduate education at Saint Louis University.

Specifically, the purposes of this investigation were to: (1) attempt to better specify factors that may be responsible for the positive ratings of graduating graduate students regarding values and ethics dimensions in their graduate education; and, (2) to solicit suggestions to better promote values and ethics in graduate education from both alumni and graduate faculty perspectives.

Method

Two surveys were developed to operationalize experiences that may underlie perceptions of graduate alumni and faculty concerning values and ethics dimensions in graduate education. Samples of these surveys were distributed to 50 potential participants and consultants seeking their assessment of survey design and content. Both surveys were modified as a result of these evaluations.

Each survey consisted of ten parallel questions that were rated on a Likert-type index ranging from "Strongly Agree" to "Strongly Disagree." A category of "Not Applicable" was included as a response choice. Three different open-ended questions appeared on the two surveys. The surveys also differed in the descriptive information requested from the participants. Alumni were asked to identify their department, major field, area of concentration, and gender. In addition, the Graduate Faculty Survey also requested information regarding years of service, types of interactions with graduate students, and sources of information contributing to their knowledge of the identity and mission of Saint Louis University.

A record search was made of the 1,189 alumni who completed the Exit Questionnaire producing addresses for 1,168, all of whom were mailed surveys. In addition, surveys were distributed to all 507 members of the Graduate Faculty. The respondent master lists and the surveys were coded on the return envelope to assist in the determination of the need for a subsequent mailing and to assure anonymous coding. Both surveys were accompanied by cover letters from the dean of the Graduate School and stamped, self-addressed envelopes were enclosed. A second request for participation was made to both categories of respondents who did not respond to the original request.

Results and Discussion

Thirty-seven percent (37%) of the alumni and fifty-five percent (55%) of the faculty responded to the survey. A thorough qualitative and quantitative analysis of the data was completed, but a complete presentation of these results is beyond the scope of this paper. In summary, the descriptive statistics support the hypothesis that personal interactions among faculty, staff, and students, and the perception of the departments' commitment to respect for students, and to gender, racial and ethnic equality, constitute the strongest predictors of satisfaction. The extensive comments made by alumni and faculty further support this hypothesis. While the qualitative data needed to be reduced because of their magnitude and to retain confidentiality, the evaluation of these comments strongly supports the importance of the concept of Jesuit humanism and faculty/student interaction, and the commitment demonstrated by the personal example of the faculty and staff.

The faculty qualitative data are even more positive in the support of this assumption. It is important, however, to note that there was a statistically significant difference between the ratings of the alumni and the faculty, suggesting that the graduate faculty respondents, as a whole, may perceive that they are doing a better job of instilling values and ethics in their graduate students than the students perceive.

The research results provided positive alumni and faculty perceptions of the impact of Jesuit humanism and campus culture on the education of the whole person at the graduate level. Suggestions to enhance values and ethics dimensions in graduate education were provided by both groups of respondents. A complete copy of this study may be obtained by contacting Dr. Donald G. Brennan, Dean of the Graduate School/Associate Provost for Research, Saint Louis University, 3663 Lindell Blvd., Suite 100, St. Louis, MO 63108.

About the Editors

John F. Kavanaugh, S.J. is Professor of Philosophy and Director of the Ethics Across the Curriculum Program at Saint Louis University. Fr. Kavanaugh was ordained a priest in the Society of Jesus in 1971 and received his doctorate in Social Philosophy from Washington University in St. Louis in 1974. He has frequently lectured and published on issues of consumerism, American culture, advertising, community and resistance, social justice, intrinsic value, and the ethics of life (euthanasia, abortion, war). He is the author of several books, including most recently *Faces of Poverty, Faces of Christ* (Orbis Books); *The Word Embodied: Meditations on the Sunday Scriptures* (Orbis Books); and *Who Count as Persons and May We Kill Them?* (Georgetown University Press). Fr. Kavanaugh is a regular columnist for *America* magazine, an award- winning syndicated columnist, and the recipient of numerous awards for teaching excellence.

Donna J. Werner is a doctoral candidate in Philosophy and Program Coordinator for the Ethics Across the Curriculum Program at Saint Louis University. She also serves as Adjunct Faculty in Philosophy and in the School of Business MBA Program. Ms. Werner earned her B.S. in Business Administration with an emphasis in Accounting from University of Missouri–St. Louis in 1986. After several years of working in the defense industry, she returned to school and earned her M.A. in Philosophical Studies at Southern Illinois University at Edwardsville. She is the recipient of SIUE's Robert Gray Memorial Award in Philosophy for Leadership and Scholarship and Saint Louis University Graduate Student Association's Outstanding Teaching Award.

About the Contributors

Michael D. Barber, S.J., **Ethics Is an Optics**
Michael Barber is Professor of Philosophy at Saint Louis University. He received his B.A. and M.A. from Saint Louis University, his M.Div. from Loyola of Chicago, and his Ph.D. from Yale. Author of over 25 articles, he has written books on the philosophies of Alfred Schutz (Bucknell University Press) and Max Scheler (Bucknell) and on

Enrique Dussel's Philosophy of Liberation (Fordham), as well as a fourth book, forthcoming, *Equality and Alterity: Phenomenological Investigations of Prejudice* (Prometheus Press). His pastoral work as a Jesuit priest includes service to the Hispanic and African-American communities in Fairmont City, Illinois and St. Louis.

Robert Bolla, Ethical Issues in Undergraduate Education: A Biologist's View

Robert Bolla, Professor and Chairperson of Biology at Saint Louis University, received his M.A. and Ph.D. from University of Massachusetts–Amherst. His distinguished teaching career includes appointments at University of Missouri–St. Louis and Washington University. He serves as associate editor of the *Journal of Nematology* and a reviewer for several professional journals and associations. He is president-elect of the Society of Nematologists. Among his more than 75 publications are studies in molecular and genetic mechanisms of plants for resistance to parasitic nematodes and his current research focuses on molecular genetic studies of the resistance of soybean to soybean cyst nematode.

Donald G. Brennan, Alumni and Faculty Perceptions of Values and Ethics in Graduate Education at Saint Louis University

Donald Brennan received his Bachelor's and Master's degrees in Speech-Language Pathology and Audiology from Saint Louis University and his Ph.D. in Communication Sciences and Disorders from the University of Oklahoma Medical Center. Dr. Brennan has served in numerous administrative and leadership roles in hospitals, community clinical facilities, and in higher education. He has held his current position as Dean of the Graduate School and Associate Provost for Research at Saint Louis University for the last twelve years.

Mark Chmiel, Three Essentials in Undergraduate Education

Mark Chmiel is Adjunct Faculty in the Theology Department of Saint Louis University and at the Aquinas Institute of Theology in St. Louis. Dr. Chmiel received his doctorate from the Graduate Theological Union in Berkeley. Having taught and written in the areas of social justice, the Holocaust, and global ethics, his book *Elie Wiesel and the Politics of Solidarity* is forthcoming from Temple University Press.

James E. Fisher, **Making Choices: Teaching Business Ethics**

James Fisher, Director of the Emerson Electric Center for Business Ethics and Associate Professor of Marketing at Saint Louis University, received his M.Div. from Yale University and his Ph.D. in Business Administration (Marketing) from the University of Illinois, Champaign–Urbana. His teaching responsibilities have focused in the area of marketing management, buyer behavior, and business ethics. His published research and consulting have focused on household spending patterns, social class influences, and consumer satisfaction.

Judith L. Gibbons, **Attention to Vulnerability as a Condition for a University Community Committed to Ethical Treatment of Others**

Judith Gibbons, Professor of Psychology at Saint Louis University, received her M.S. and Ph.D. in psychology from Carnegie-Mellon University. She is widely respected for her teaching abilities and is the recipient of both the Nancy McNeir Ring Award for Outstanding Contribution as a Teacher and the Missouri Governor's Award for Excellence in Teaching. She is co-founder and past director of the Women's Studies Program at Saint Louis University. Her research has produced more than 70 publications on issues ranging from cross-cultural ideals of adolescents to the connection between brain chemistry and behavior.

James F. Gilsinan, **Ethics and Public Service**

James Gilsinan, Dean of the College of Public Service at Saint Louis University, received his doctorate in Sociology from the University of Colorado after having acquired earlier degrees from Loyola University of Chicago. He is highly regarded as a teacher, having received the Nancy McNair Ring Award for Outstanding Contribution as a Teacher. His major works, *Criminology and Public Policy: An Introduction* (Prentice Hall) and *Doing Justice: How the System Works—as seen by the participants* (Prentice Hall), have been complemented by an array of scholarly articles, major grants, and wide consulting work in criminal justice and the penal system.

Sharon M. Homan, **What's Ethics Got to Do with Public Health? Fostering Professional Ethics and Social Responsibility in Public Health**

Sharon Homan, Associate Professor and Director of the Division of Biostatistics with the School of Public Health at Saint Louis University, received her M.S. in Preventive Medicine and Ph.D. in Biostatistics from the University of Iowa. She also has appointments in the Department of Public Policy and the Center for Health Care Ethics at Saint Louis University as well as the Urban Family and Community Development Program at Washington University's School of Social Work. Homan is the Director of the St. Louis Faith and Health Consortium, in partnership with the Carter Center of Emory University. Her teaching, publications, and grant research have concentrated on rural poverty, family health, public housing, chemical dependence, and "faith and health."

Sandra H. Johnson, **The Interface of Law, Medicine, and Ethics**

Sandra Johnson is Provost of Saint Louis University and Professor of Law at the Center for Health Law Studies with joint appointments at the School of Medicine and School of Public Health. A former President of the American Society of Law, Medicine and Ethics, Professor Johnson is a Fellow of the Hastings Center, the co-author of numerous scholarly volumes, as well as articles in *JAMA* and the *New England Journal of Medicine*, and a national presence, through lecturing, consulting, and leadership in the field of Health Care Law. Professor Johnson received her B.A. from Saint Louis University, her J.D. from New York University, and her LL.M. from Yale Law School.

James H. Korn, **Teaching the Ethics of Teaching**

James Korn, Professor of Psychology at Saint Louis University since 1974, received his M.S. and Ph.D. from Carnegie-Mellon University. In 1995, he was the G. Stanley Hall Lecturer for the American Psychological Association. Among his more than 40 publications are studies in memory, teaching excellence, and ethics in the research with humans. In 1997, he published *Illusions of Reality: A History of Deception in Social Psychology* (State University of New York Press).

Gerard Magill, **Ethics in Health Sciences Education**

Gerard Magill is the Department Chair and Director of the Center for Health Care Ethics at Saint Louis University. With earlier degrees in Philosophy and Moral Theology from the Gregorian University in Rome, he received his Ph.D. in Ethics from Edinburgh University in Scotland. In addition to 23 years in graduate education, Dr. Magill has edited major works on values and public life, abortion, and assisted suicide; written 26 scholarly essays; and secured significant grant awards for Saint Louis University. He has a forthcoming book: *Imagination and Responsibility*

Avis E. Meyer, **Ethics Across the Curriculum: It Is working**
Avis Meyer, Professor in the Department of Communication, received his Ph.D. from Saint Louis University. Nominated for the Burlington Northern Teaching Award three times, he was given the Nancy McNeir Ring Award for Outstanding Contribution as a Teacher in 1985. In 1990, an alumni survey identified him as one of the ten most "memorable, influential and effective teachers" at Saint Louis University. The Student Life Advising Award has been named after him since 1994. For 25 years he has served as advisor to the *University News*, one of the most honored college weeklies in the country. His articles have appeared in *Journalism Educator*, the *Nieman Foundation Reports*, the *Flannery O'Connor Bulletin*, and the *St. Louis Post-Dispatch*.

Ronald E. Modras, **Alumni and Faculty Perceptions of Values and Ethics in Graduate Education at Saint Louis University**
Ronald Modras is a Professor of Theological Studies at Saint Louis University. He received his doctorate from the University of Tübingen, Germany. His publications include several books, most recently *The Catholic Church and Antisemitism: Poland, 1933–1939*, which was named the 1994 book of the year by the College Theology Society. In 1989, he was named a Fellow of the Annenberg Research Institute (Philadelphia, PA). He is listed in the *International Who's Who in Education* and other biographic listings.

Dennis J. Tuchler, **What Has Ethics Got to Do with Teaching Law?**
Dennis Tuchler, Professor of Law at Saint Louis University since 1971, received his B.A. from Reed College and his J.D. from the University of Chicago. Professor Tuchler has written articles on professional responsibility, conflict of laws, local government law, and appellate procedure. He received a fellowship from the National Endowment for the Humanities to participate in their Summer Humanities Seminar and has lectured at the Ruhr University in Bochum, Germany. He teaches Legal Profession, Legislation, Remedies, and Conflict of Laws. He also teaches seminars on the Legal Profession.

Joya Uraizee, **The Role of Ethics in the Undergraduate Curriculum**

Joya Uraizee received her doctorate in Postcolonial English Literature from Purdue, after an earlier M.A. from Baylor and a B.A. from Saint Xavier's College in Calcutta. Since 1994 she has taught Comparative Literature, Post-Colonial Voices, Black Voices, and World Literature in the English Department at Saint Louis University. Among her publications are chapters in *Black Women Across Cultures* and *Writing the Nation: Self and Country in the Post-colonial Imagination*. Dr. Uraizee serves on the Women's Studies Core Committee and the African-American Studies Advisory Board.